Bezüglich
regarding

Fehlern
mistakes

die
the, f

Rechtschreibung
spelling

betreffend
concerning

können
can

Sie
you, formal

mich
me

über
through. via

den
the

Verlag
publishing company

„Book
Buch

on
auf

Demand
Anfrage

GmbH"
(Ltd.)

oder
or

möglicherweise
possibly

unter
under

JederAufenthal@posteo.de
[e-mail-adress]

kontaktieren,
contact, *verb*

aber
but

ob
whether

ich
I

antworten
answer, verb

werde,
will, verb

liegt
lies, position, figurative

im
in

Bereich
area

der
of

Spekulation.
speculation.

Dass
That

das
the, n

„S"
big S in quotation marks

fast
almost

aussieht
looks, *passive*

wie
like

eine
a

‚fünf'
five

ist
is

die
the

Schwäche
weakness

dieser
of this

Schriftart
font

mit
with

dem
the

Namen
name

„Exo
[name

2":
name]

5S5S5S5S5S5S5S..
5S5S5S5S5S5S5S..

ich
I

distanziere
distance, verb

mich
me

von
of

dieser
this

Nachlässigkeit
carelessness

(Häuptling
chief

blinkender
flashing

Cursor
Cursor

darf
may

natürlich
naturally

nicht
not

fehlen)
to be absent

Schriftart:
font

Exo2,
[name]

zu
to

finden
find

unter
under

https://fonts.google.com/ specimen/Exo+2
[adress]

(*zuletzt
last, time. order

abgerufen
retrieved

am
the, date

27.
27.

September
september

2024),
2024

lizenziert
licensed

mit
with
der
the

Open
offen

Font
Schriftart

License
Lizenz

4

https://openfontlicense.org/*
[adress]

Knüsterl':
~ artist, atirts

Jeder
every

Aufenthal
[name]

Schreibknecht:
writing servant

Auf
on

einem
a

mit
with

Linux
linux

betriebenen,
run

generalstabsmäßig
in manner of generals staff

überholten
overhauled

ThinkPad-Klapprechner
Thinkpad-folding calculator

verfasst.
written

Künstliche-Intelligenz- Befürchgtungs-gegenrede:
artificial intelligence fear counter speech

Automatisierte
automated

Analysen
analyzes

dieses
of this

Werkes
work, noun

sind
are

nicht
not

gewünscht
wished, desired

respektive
respectively

mit
with

Hinweis
indication, clue

auf
to

geltendes
valid, applieable

Recht
right

untersagt,
forbidden

auch
as well, > > even

wenn
if

dadurch
~ through, by, thus

nur
only

Informationen
informations

über
over

Muster
patterns

Trends
trends

und
and

Korrelationen
correlations

Vorwort
preface

Buch
book

Übersetzung
Translation

Über
above

Setzen
to seat

Wörterbuch
dictionary

Problem
problem

Lösung
solution

Lösung
dissolution

chemische Lösung
dissolution

wässrige Lösung
fluid, „watery" solution

Postmoderne
post-modernity

Moderne
modernity

Epoche
era

Vergleich
Comparison

Finden
find

Suchen
to look for

Mensch,
human

Reling,
deck rail

Platsch
spalsh

The goof life
Das gute Leben

Lücke
gap

Mind the gap
Achten Sie auf die Lücke
zwischen Trittschiene und
Bahnsteigkante

geschrieben | übersetzt
written | translated

von
by

und
and

zu
of / to / ~ in

Jeder
[name]

Aufenthal
[name]

Graf
count

der
of the

Lordschaft
Lordship

Sichkaput
[name]

in
in

Bundes'
federal

Berlejen
[name], variation of ‚Berlin'

Platzhalter
place holder

ISBN
978-3-7693-0234-9

**BIBLIOGRAFISCHE
INFORMATION DER
DEUTSCHEN
NATIONALBIBLIOTHEK:**
Die Deutsche
Nationalbibliothek verzeichnet
diese Publikation in der
Deutschen
Nationalbibliografie;
detaillierte bibliografische
Daten sind im Internet über
http://dnb.dnb.de abrufbar.

textbf{UMSCHLAGGESTALTUN
G:}\\
Martin Ehrhardt\\

~~**TATSÄCHLICHER TITEL:**~~
~~Mann, Reling, Bord~~

URHEBERRECHT:
© 2024 Jeder Aufenthal,
Martin Ehrhardt (Hrsg.)

Verlag:
BoD · Books on Demand GmbH,
In de Tarpen 42, 22848
Norderstedt

Druck:
Libri Plureos GmbH,
Friedensallee 273, 22763
Hamburg

\setcounter{page}{1}
\\

Abk. Abkürzung
abbr. Abbreviation

In case of mistakes or assumed spell misopportunities, please do not hesitate to contact the publishing company named on the first page in order to collect the corrections in order to set up a second Auflage.

The empty pages in the original work are caused by the wish that every ‚cahpter', named „Zäsur" in german, which might be a new manner, to bring a structure into texts, begins at the top left of a two pages aperçu. It's like a menu in a restaurant, but please do not confuse your nutrition with your mental support.

If you desire to translate the book, please contact ~~the white house~~ the german federal government in order to contact me ~~or to execute your wish on ‚Staats Nacken' as we are able to name it in german without giving credit to the leaders pres'dent and chancellor, mainly appearing in the public scenery.~~ The current pres'dent ~~Biden giveth a number — +1 203 404 0880 — on his Instagram page where you can write your deepest wishes to but potentially you might be able to use that opportunity~~ a little more cleverly. Also, ~~I'd like to inform you,~~ no matter what circumstance ~~leads to the fact that you read theese text, that we know how to name the trace~~ a rabbit leaves ~~if fleeing — and that some~~, might contain traces of false friends, thus wrong translations but I believe you're able to figure out the intentions~~, to~~ to find a good translation on your own!

Botschaft
Message, Ambassy

Germany
Deutschland

gemäß
according

§44b
§44b

UrhG
abbr. Copyright law

(„Text
text

und
and

Data
data

Mining")
mining

gewonnen
won

gespeichert
saved, memory

aber
but

nicht
not

verarbeitet
processed

werden
to become, to be

sollen
~ shall

Dem
To this

entgegenstehende
~ contradicting

Vorhaben
intentions, plans

können
can, are able to
Sie
you, *formal*

bis
until

auf
on

weiteres
further

JederAufenthal@posteo.de
[adress]

mitteilen
tell, message, tp adress to

Bibliografische
~ bibliographic

Information
information

der
of the

Deutschen
german

Nationalbibliothek
national library

Die
the, female

Deutsche
german

Nationalbibliothek
national library

verzeichnet
records, *verb*

diese
~ theese

Publikation
publication

in
in

der
the

Deutschen
german

Nationalbibliografie
national bibliography

detaillierte
detailed

bibliografische
~ libraric

Daten
data

sind
are

im
in

Internet
internet

über
over, ‚via'

http://dnb.dnb.de
[adress]

abrufbar
retrieveable

Umschlaggestaltung:
cover design

Jeder
every

Aufenthal;
~ On-a-valley

(Das
the

Bild
picture

vom
of the

Brandenburger
brandenburg

Tor
gate

stammt
originates

von
of, from

Martin
[name]

Ehrhardt,
[name]

aber	**Demand**	**Druck**
but	Anfrage	print, pressure
nur	**GmbH**	**auf**
only	~ Ltd.	on
die	**Norderstedt,**	**Anfrage**
the	[name]	demand
Auslösung	**https://www.bod.de**	**(Häuptling**
trigger triggering (camera)	[adress]	chief
Tatsächlicher	**Druckerei:**	**blinkender**
actual	printing plant	blinking
Titel	**Libri**	**Cursor**
title	[name]	cursor
Mann,	**Plureos**	
Man	[name]	**verfolgt**
Reling,	**GmbH, Friedensallee**	follows
Deck Rail	Ltd., [street name]	**den**
Bord	**Hamburg**	the
Board, *naut.*	[name]	**Text**
Urheberrecht:	**Internationale**	text
copyright	international	**sehr**
©	**Standard-BuchNummer**	very, quite
[thing]	standard book number	**genau)**
2024	**„ISBN":**	precise
2024	=	**ich**
Jeder	**978-3-7583-4036-9**	I
every single	=	**suche**
Aufenthal.	**Neunbillionensiebenhundertdr**	look
stya, *noun*	**eiundachtzigmillardensiebenh**	**nach**
Ansprechbare	**underdachtundfünfzigmillione**	for
responsive	**ndreihundertvierzigtausenddr**	
Druckerbande:	**eihundertneunundsechzig**	**einem**
printing gang	nine trillion	a
Verlag:	sevenhundredandthree billion	
publishing company	sevenhundredandfiftyeight million	**Programm,**
BoD	threehundredfourtythousand	program
[name]/abbreviation	threehundredsixtynine	**mit**
Books	**Bisher**	with
Bücher	up to now	**dem**
on	**einzige**	the
auf	solely	**man**
	Auflage	one
	circulation	

Text
text

verarbeiten
process, verb

kann
can

Inhalt
content

Erste
first

Zäsur
~ turning point

Das
the

Hafenbecken
harbor basin

hat
has

einen
a

Promillewert.
alcohol level

Zweite
second

Zäsur
~ turning point

Ich
I

stehe
stand

an
at

Deck,
deck

weil
because
ich
I

an
at

Deck
deck

stehe.
stand.

Dritte
third

Zäsur
turning point

Die
the

Reling
deck rail

hat
has

Eigenschaften.
attributes

Vierte
fourth

Zäsur
~ turning point

Es
it

sind
are

mehrere
multiple

Schiffe
ships

die
which

sind
are

aber
but

verschieden
differently
orientiert
orientated

Nur
only

manche
some

fliegen
fly

stur
stubborn

gen'
towards

Himmel.
sky

Wievielte
howmuchs, neologism

Zäsur
turning point

Das
The

Mitzählen
count with, during occurance
of counteable, ~ \include

ist
is

zwar
~ indeed

gestattet,
allowed

aber
but

es
it

stört
disturbs

beim
in, during

Nachdenken
Thinking, overthinking: often
after an event or situation
Sechste
sixth

Zäsur
turning point

Pontons
pontoon

sind
are

relevant
relevant
für
for

Schiffe
ships

und
and

für
for

Kreuzfahrten
cruises.

Siebente
seventh

Zäsur
turning point

Das
the

Untergehen
sinking

ist
is

Schiffen
ships, to

nicht
not

untersagbar
forbiddeable, neologism

Achte
eighth

Zäsur
turning point / cut

Rote
red

Fäden
threads

sind
are

schwer
hard

zu
to

finden
find

aber
but

immer
always, *usually*

rot
red

Neunte
ninth

Zäsur
cut, caesoor

Relingen
deck rails

sind
are

nur
only

statisch
statically

stabil
stable

funktional
functional

Zehnte
tenth

Zäsur
turning point

Rufen
call, courtesly
Sie
you, *formal*

laut
loud

„**Ich**
»I

genehmige
authorize

die
the

Produktion
production

von
of

Konservendosen"
conserving tin cans«

Elfte
eleventh

Zäsur
cut

Ich
I

fördere
support

die
the, *female*

Umbenennung
renaming

Berlins
berlins

in
in

»Berlejen«.
[name]

Zwölfte
twelveth

Zäsur
caesur

Die
the, f

Kombüse
galley

ist
is

abseits
offsite

der
the, genitiv case

Reling.
Deck rail

Dreizehnte
thirteenth

Zäsur
turning point

Wasser
water

ist
is

ein
a

vorzügliches,
excellent

aber
but

nicht
not

immer
always

hinreichendes
sufficient, *math.*

Getränk.
Drink, object

Vierzehnte
fourteenth

Zäsur
tipping point

»Das
»The one

mit
with

der
the

Schreibblockade"
writing blockade«

Zäsur
turning point, cut and caesur

fünfzehn
fifteen

Dies
This, thees

ist
is

kein
no, not a

Märchen,
tale

ich
I

wiederhole:
repeat

dies
this

ist
is

kein
no

Märchen
tale

Zäsur
turning point

sechzehn
sixteen

Die
the

Kommunikation
communication

war
was

fast
almost

noch
still

nie
never

zuvor
before

auf
on

der
the

Ebene
level

des
of, *genitiv case*

binären
binary

Zahlensystems
number system

angelangt
arrived

Siebzehnte
seventeenth

Zäsur
caesur

Das
That

war
was

mein
my

Fehler
mistake, *also behavioural*

Achtzehnte
eightteenth

Zäsur
caesur

Finden
find

Sie
you, *formal*

einen
a

Kanzlerkandidaten
chancellor-candidate

auf
on („auffinden")

verweisen
redirect

Sie
you, *formal*

ihn
him, *relational*

bitte
please

an
to

eine
a

Partei
Party, Partei

Neunzehnte
nineteenth

Zäsur
caesur

Wählen
elect

Sie
you

Korintha
[name]

Geringa-Geringcko
[name]-[name]

Zwanzigste
twentiest

Zäsur
caesur
Man
One, someone

kann
can

sich
oneself

auch
as well as, too ,equally

auf
on

ein
a

Thema
theme

fokussieren
to focus

Einundzwanzigste
oneandtwentiest

Zäsur
turning point

keine
no

Angaben
statement

das
that

ist
is

aber
but

auch
also

ein
a

ruhiger
silent, quiet

Dienstag
thursday

Zweiundzwanzigste
twentysecond

Zäsur
caesur

Bücher
books

müssen
must

nicht
not

mehr
more, any more

gedruckt
printed

werden
to be, to become

Dreiundzwanzigste
twentythird

Zäsur
turning point, cut

Verschachtelungen
~>> the onion

führen
lead

nicht
not

immer
always

zum
to

Tod
death

Vierundzwanzigste
fourandtwentiest

Zäsur
caesur

»Das
»The
Buch«
book«

Fümmunzwanzigste
twentyfifth

Zäsur
turning point

Auch
as well as

das
the

Wasser
water

knapp
meagre

oberhalb
above

des
the, *genitiv case*

Hafenbeckenbodens
harbour basin ground

hat
has

einen
a

Promillewert.
blood alcoohol level

Sečhsundzwanzigste
26th

Zæsur
turning point, cut

Kafkas
Kafka's

Werk
work, noun

war
was

unvollendet
unfinished, incomplete

und
and
das
the

obige
above

»čh«
»ß«

möchte
would like to

ich
I

als
as

frigativlaut
frigative sound, scratchy
sound

interpretiert
interpreted

wissen
to know

Zäsur
caesur

Siebenundzwanzig   ~
27

Testtest,
testtest

Ende
end

des
of the, *genitiv case*

Buchs
book

Bonusseite
bonus page

Malen
paint

Sie
you, formal
eine
a

Ente
duck
Bonusseite
bonus page

Kreieren
create

Sie
you, *formal*

eine
a

technische
technical

Zeichnung
drawing

Bonusseite
bonus page

Kreieren
create

Sie
you, *formal*

eine
a

weitere
further

technische
technical

Zeichnung
drawing

über
above, spanning over

zwei
two

Seiten
pages

hinweg
over, spanning over

Bonusseite
bonus page
Kreieren
create

Sie
you

eine
a

weitere
further

technische
technical

Zeichnung
drawing

über
over

zwei
two

Seiten
pages

hinweg
away

Hier
here

an
on

Deck
deck

des
of the

Schiffes
ship

ist's
is it, *isit*

schön
beautifully

licht
bright, lightful, no shadows

Partout
everywhere, *orig. french*

stehen
stand

bunte
colourful

Rettungsringe
lifebelt, spare tire

an
at

die
the, feminin

Fußböden
floor, foot floor

gelehnt
leant

und
and

die
the

Bordwände
bordwall

leuchten
shine

vor
of

Glück
luck

Eine
A

fremde
strange

Frau
Woman

kommt
cometh

auf
on

mich
me

zu
to

und
and

stiehlt
steals

mir
me

mein
my

Sektglas
Sparkling wine glas

Nichts
nothing

ist
is

so,
just, as, like

wie
as, like

ich
I

es
it

mir
me

vorstelle
Imagine.

„Auf
„On

Wiedersehen"
Review" [good bye]

brülle
roar

ich
I

in
in

mich
me

hinein
into

„Sie
„You

wollen
want

mir
me, *reflective*

gerne
~ gladly

ein
a

volles
full

Sektglas
champaign glass

wiederbringen",
to return", to bring back"

flüstere
whisper

ich
I

ihr
her

Seite | page 1

13

ins
in the

Ohr
ear

als
when

sie
she

an
at

mir
me

vorbeigeht.
Passes.

Die
The, f

fremde
strange

Frau
Woman

ohne
without

Namensschild
name shield

steht
stands

direkt
directly

vor
before, in front of

mir
mee

als
when

ich
I

sie
her

nach
towards

ihrem
her

Namen
name

frage
ask

den
the

sie
she

nicht
not

zu
to

kennen
know

angibt
States, gives

„Sie
„She

müssen
must

noch
still

das
the

Schiff
ship

taufen",
baptemize«,

sagt
says

sie
she

und
and

händigt
hands out

mir
to me, mee

eine
a

Flasche
bottle

'89er
'89

Mauerfallchampagner
Champagne of falling wall,
Wallfallchampagne

aus
from

„aber
„but

die
the

Situation
situation

sei
would be

schade
unfortunate

um
regarding, ~*around*

den
the

Sekt."
sparkling wine."

Mit
With

klerikalem
clerical

Habitus
habitus, behaviour, conduct

schleudere
fling, hurl

ich
I

die
the

14

Flasche
bottle

über
over

die
the

Reling
deck rail

und
and

rufe
call

„daneben!".
„besides!".

Der
the

Sekt
sparkling wine

fällt
falls

ins, *in das*
into the

Wasser
water

und
and

ein
a

Blick
Look

an
at

Deck
deck

bestätigt
confirms

den
the

Erfolg
success

der
the, genitiv case

Aktion,
action

wo
where

Maschinisten
machinists

in
in

blauen
blue

Latzhosen
work trousers, dungarees;
overalls, but arms free

neue
new

Klebefolien
sticking foil

an
at

den
the

Bordwänden
bord walls

der
of the, genitiv case

MS
motor ship, abbreviation of
„Motorschiff"

daneben
next to it, besides

anbringen
attatch

Tatsächlich
actual

erscheinen
appear

die
the

Maschinisten
machinists

wie
as, like

in
in

einem
a

Cartoon
cartoon

mit
with

kleinen
small

Rändern
bordures, edges

um
around

die
the

Konturen
contour, outline

und
and

ohne
without

Schattierung
shading

der
of the, at the

sie
them, these

umgebenden
surrounding

Flächen
areas

Mit
With

Blick
Regard

auf
on

das
the

monströse
monstrous

Hafengelände
harbour bassin

tippele
to walk silently on toes

ich
I

auf
on

der
the

Stelle
Site, place

Mein
My

Blick
Look

schweift
wanders, sweeps, roams

nüchtern
soberly

über
over

die
the

Anlagen
facilities, plants

die
which

gestapelt
stacked

sind
are

wie
like

kleine
small

Container
containers

in
in

Hafengebäuden
harbour buildings

auf
on

denen
theese

die
the

Flagge
flag

der
of the

Seestreitkräfte
marine combat forces

der
of the

Deutschen
german

Demokratischen
democratic

Republik
republic

weht. *flattert*
waves, flutters

Das
The

Haupt, *Kopf*
Main, *head*

Meiner
Of my

ziert
decorates, adorns

eine
an

amerikanische
american

Baseballmütze
baseball cap

aus
from

dem
the

Jahre
year, *a little formal (Jahr)*

2024,
2024,

die
the

per
through, via

Zeitschaltuhr
timer

bereits
already

in
in

das
the

Jahr
year

2045
2045

gereist
traveled

war
was

und
and

erschöpft
exhausted

wieder
again

zurückkehrte
returned

Ich
I

lerne
learned

wie
how

man
one

an
at

der
the

Reling
deck rail

steht
stands

und
and

entnehme
retrieve

einer
a

spontan
spontaneously

auftauchenden
appearing

Zigarettendose
cigarette tin can, box

das
the

Mikrofon,
microphone

über
above

das
which

Ich
I

fortan
~ henceforth ~

spontan
spontaneously

Durchsagen
announcements

an
to, at

das
the

gesamte
whole

Schiff
ship

sende:
send

„Sehr
„Very

geehrter
honored

Herr
Lord, man

Kapitän,
captain

die
the

'MS
„MS

daneben'
besides

befindet
finds

sich
itself

genau
exactly

im
in the

Hafen
harbour

und
and

ich
I

bitte
ask, *please*

Sie
you, *formal*

nun
now

endlich
finally

zu
to

sinken
sink

Wir
we

haben
have

schließlich
after all, *finally (reasoning)*

viel
much

Geld
money

bezahlt
spent

Um
In order to

das
that

Statement
statement

zu
to

unterstreichen
underline, *figurative*

entnehme
retrieve, extract, take out

ich
I

meinem
(of) my

Sakko
jacket

ein
a

Bündel
bundle

diverser
[of] diverse

Devisen
foreign currency

und
and

werfe
throw

sie
them

über
over

Bord
board

„Jetzt
„Now

sofort
now, immediately

sinken!",
sink!",

füge
append

ich
I

an.
< < append: anfügen

Ein
A

Zylinder
cylinder

des
of the, *genitif case*

Schiffsmotors
ship motor

steht
stands

neben
beside

weiteren
further

Zylindern
cylinders

unter
under

einer
a

großen
big

Welle,
wave,

die
which

außerhalb
outside

des
the

Schiffes
ship

beständig
steadily

angeliefert
delivered

wird
is, *process*

und
and

ist
is

im
in

Grundriss
ground plan

rund,
round

aber
but

im
in the, in its

Querschnitt
cross section

nicht
not

Wird
~ Is being

Wasser
water

an
a

Bord
board

gepumpt,
pumped,

dienen
serve

die
the

Zylinder
cylinders

als
as

Lagerraum
storage rooms

Die
The

Gäste
guests

kippen
tilt

ihre
their

mit
with

Seewasser
sea water

gefüllten
filled, state

Sektgläser
sparkling wine glasses

in
in, into

die
the

Zylinder
cylinders

von
from

wo
where

aus
~ from

sie
they

dann
then

auslaufen.
set sail, drain out, run empty,
leak

Manchmal
Sometimes

werden
are being

Zylinder
cylinders

bei
during

Feierlichkeiten
celebrations, *formal*

an
on, at, a

Bord
board

benötigt
needed, ~ ennecessitied ~

beispielsweise
as an example

bei
during
einem
a

Maschinenschaden
machine damage

Der
The

falsche
wrong

Passagier
passenger

an
a, at

Bord
board

der
the

„MS
„MS

daneben"
besides"

ist
is

nicht
not

etwa
about, around

eine
a

Person
person

ohne
without

Fahrschein
ticket

sondern
but, instead

diejenige,
the one, female

die
which, the, *female*

eigentlich
actually

am
at the

wenigsten
most minimal, least

mitfahren
ride with

wollte
wanted

aber
but

der
the

Gruppenzwang
group-obligation

gebietete
~ ordered, forced to

es
it

nunmal.
„nowonce", indicating a not
variable circumstance
invariant, fix

Dass
That

der
the

falsche
wrong

Passagier
passenger

direkt
directly

neben
beside

mir
me

auf
on

der
the

anderen
other

Seite
Side

der
of the

Reling
deck rail

stand
stood

verwunderte
~ wondered

mich
me

nur
only

ein
a

wenig
little.

Eine
A, an

alte
old

Englischlehrerin
english teacher, female

bereitete
prepared

ihren
her
Unterricht
lessons

vor
pre (prepare)

und
and

mit
with

der
the

anderen
other

Gehirnhälfte
cerebral hemisphere

die
which, the

sie
they

an
at

Bord
board

gelagert
stored

hatte
had

korrigierte
corrected, 3.person singular

sie
she

Duplikate
duplicates

alter
of old

Shakespeare-Handschriften.
Shakespeare-handwritings.

Ihr
Her

Erscheinungsbild
Appearance

ist
is

transparent
transparent

die
the

Deckkraft
opacity, covering power

liegt
lies

wohl
~ apparently, *a little uncertain*

bei
at

etwa
around

Prozent:
percent

man
one

kann
can

durch
through

sie
them

hindurchsehen,
watch through

und
and

sobald
as soon as

ich
I

das
that

tat
did

verschwand disappeared	**auf** on	**wieder** again
sie she	**der** the	**hinter** behind
auch also	**Brücke** bridge	**mir** me
wieder again	**verschwinden.** disappear.	**auftauchte** appeared
Ich I	**Von** From	**und** and
bat asked	**dort** there	**sah** saw
sie her	**unten** down	**durch** through
die the	**konnte** could	**seine** his
Sektflasche champaign bottle	**sie** she	**Uniform** uniform
aus from	**den** the	**hindurch** through
dem the	**Untergang** sinking	**dass** that
Hafenwasser harbour water	**gut** good	**seine** his
zu to	**mitbekommen.** notice.	**Gänsehaut** goosebumps
fischen fish	**Der** The	**einem** a
und and	**Kapitän** captain	**Robbenfell** ~ seal pell
ließ let'	**grüßte** greeted	**wich** passed its place
sie her	**die** the	**was** which, what
in in	**Englischlehrerin,** english teacher,	**das** the
einem a	**die** the	**Zeichen** sign
Rettungsring life belt	**plötzlich** suddenly	**für** for

ihn
him

war
was

sofort
immediately

den
the

Reifendruck
tire air pressure

zu
to

überprüfen
check

Dafür
For this

schickte
sent

er
he

seinen
his

ersten
first

Offizier
officer

in
in, *into*

den
the

Maschinenraum
machine room

um
for, *in order to, for him to*

Kohle
coal

in
into, *in*

die
the
Zylinder
cylinder

zu
to

schippen
to shovel

die
which

dafür
for that

vor
before

jeder
every

Explosion
explosion

auseinandergebaut
disassembled

und
and

aufwändig
laborious, time-conssumingly

wieder
again

zusammengesetzt
assembled

werden
to be, become

mussten
had to, *musted*

Der
The

Offizier
officer

erhielt
received

dafür
therefore, for this

später
later

eine
one

Minute
minute

Urlaub
vacation

die
the

vom
of

Typ
type

am
at

Tresen
desk, counter, bar

bezahlt
paid

wurde
was

und
and

durch
through

die
the

Gallionsfigur
figure head

mit
with

einem
a

sanften
soft, gentle

Lächeln
smile

quittiert
resigned, left, *french orig.*

ward'.
Was, *elderly german*
Erste
First

Zäsur
Zäsur

Das
The

Hafenbecken
harbour bassin

hat
has

einen
a

Promillewert
Blood alcohol value

Das
The

Wetter
wether

über
above

der
the

»MS
»MS

daneben«
next to it«

war
was

immer
always

schlecht,
bad,

außer
apart from

es
it

war
was

gut,
good,

dann
then

wurde
was

es
it

schlechter:
more bad, ~ worse ~

Regen
rain

bis
until

der
the

Pool
pool

an
at

Deck
deck

gefüllt
filled

war,
was,

dann
then

trockene
more dry, arid

Hitze
heat

bis
until

die
the

Sektgläser
sparkling wine glasses

ausgetrocknet
dried

waren,
were,

dann
then

wieder
again

Regen,
rain,

bis
until

der
the

Pool
pool

gefüllt
filled

war
was

Die
The

Matrosen
Sailors

besangen
sang to

jedes
every

Gewitter
thunderstorm

das
which

die
the

MS
MS

daneben,
beside it,

hier
here

im
in the

Hafen,
port, harbour

heimsuchte
stroke, haunted; to look for
and even until someones home

Dafür
For the named circumstance

suchten
searched

sie
she

die
the

Leuchtraketen
signalrockets, flares

entnahmen
took out

sie (Sie)
them

ohne
without

Anweisung
order,

des
of the, *genitiv*

Kapitäns
capatain

auf
on

Grundlage
basis

eines
of a

angeblichen
alleged

Notfalls,
emergency,

den
which

sie
they

sich
themselves

heimlich
secretly

gegenseitig
mutually

bestätigten
confirmed

und
and

verfolgten
followed

sich
themselves

damit
with it, with them, using them

Manchmal
Sometimes

schoss
shot

ein
a

Matrose
sailor

in
into, in

die
the

Höhe
Height

Da
As, *reason*

ich
I

der
the

Protagonist
protagonist, main figure

des
of the

Werks
work

wieder
again

an
a, at

Deck
deck

stehe
stand

entdecke
discover

ich
I

meinen
my

Willen,
will

wieder
again

an
at

Deck
deck

zu
to

stehen
stand

Zweite
second

Zäsur
Zäsur

ich
I

stehe
stand

an
at

Deck,
deck,

weil
because

ich
I

an
at

Deck
deck

stehe
Stand

Die
The

Klimaanlage
climate control

verdrängt
ousts, displaces

das
the

warme
warm

Wetter
weather

ich
I

schalte
switch

sie
it

ein
on

und
and

das
the

Wetter
weather

verschwindet.
disappeares.

Hier
Here

an
at

der
the

Reling
deck-rail

habe
have

ich
I

eine
e

gute
good

Einsicht
Insight

in
in

das
the

Leben
life

unter
under

Bord
Board

Wann
When

immer
ever

die
the

Schotten
bulkheads

passiert
passed

werden
are

das
that

sind
are

auch
also, as well

Türen
doors

in
in

einer
a

Bordwand
board wall

pfeife
whistle

ich
I

ein
a

kleines
small, little

Lied
song

in
in

der
the

antizipierten
anticipated

Nationalsprache.
national language, official language

Bevor
before

mir
to me, *mee*

das
the

Abendessen
dinner

gebracht
brough

und
and

über
over

die
the

Reling
deckrail

hinweg
over something

entsorgt
disposed

wird
is, is being, *ees*

stehe
stand

ich
I

mindestens
at least

zwei
two

weitere
further

Minuten
minutes

an
at

der
the

Reling
deckrail

und
and

denke
think

über
about

die
the

Eigenschaften
characteristics, features

der
of the

Reling
deckrail

nach *(nachdenken)*
> over[think], to think about a
event that occured in the past

Dritte
third

Zäsur
caesur

Die
The

Reling
deckrail

hat
has

Eigenschaften.
characteristics.

Bei
With

Einlasskontrollen
entry control

sind
are

die
the

Fakten
facts

eindeutig
unambiguous

haben
have

Sie
they

ein
a

Ticket
ticket

für
for

die
the

Reling
deckrail

dürfen
may

Sie
you, *formal*

an
at

der
the

Reling
deckrail

stehen
stand

Fehlt
misses, *lacks*

Ihnen
(to, of) you, *formal*

aber
but, though

das
the

Ticket
ticket

für
for

die
the

Reling
deckrail

brauchen
need

Sie
you, *formal*

ein
a

Ticket
ticket

für
for

die
the

Reling
deckrail

das
which

Sie
you, *formal*

nicht
not

an
at

der
the

Reling
deckrail

erhalten
receive

können,
can

außer
except

Sie
you, formal

stehen
stand

bereits
already

an
at

der
the

Reling
deckrail

Andernfalls
otherwise

sind
are

Sie
you, *formal*

gebeten
asked, required

fernab
apart, away, far away

der
of the, from the

Reling
deckrail

ein
a

Ticket
ticket

für
for

Seite | page 11

die
the

Reling
deckrail

zu
to

erwerben
acquire

wofür
what for

Sie
you, *formal*

Geld
money

brauchen
Need, require

Haben
Have

Sie
you, *formal*

keines
none

können
can

Sie
you

Einlasskontrolleur
entry control person

für
for

die
the

Reling
deckrail

werden
Become

Die
The

Reling
deckrail

ist
is

dann
then

für
for

Sie
you, *formal*

auch
also

nicht
not

zugänglich
accessible, entereable

Oder
or

Sie
you, *formal*

wenden
turn

sich
yourself

an
to

die
the

ErfinderInnen
Inventors, gendered

von
of

Kryptowährungen
crypto currencies

oder
or

an
at

die
the

europäische
european

Zentralbank
central bank

Dort
There

wird
is

das
the

hiesige
local

Geld
money

in
in

seiner
its

Gestalt
figure, build

gelegentlich
occasionally

erneuert
renewed

Wie
How

auf
on, in

dem
the

Dorf
village

also
so, thus

wenn
if

Sie
you, *formal*

einen
a

Stammplatz
regular, habitual place

In
in

der
the

Kirche
church

haben
have

haben
have

Sie
you, *formal*

einen
a

Stammplatz
regular seat

in
in

der
the

Kirche
church

wenn
if

aber
but

Sie
you, *formal*

keinen
no

Stammplatz
regular place, seat

haben
have

brauchen
need, require

Sie
you, *formal*

eine
a

Kirche
church

sodass
such that

Sie
you, *formal*

darin
within, in there

einen
a

Stammplatz
regular seat

haben
have

können
Can.

Sie
you, *formal*

müssen
must

also
as wel

Ihren
your

Stammplatz
regular seat, place

den
which

Sie
you

nicht
not

haben
have

gegen
against

Kenntnisse
knowledges

im
in

Kirchenbau
curch construction

tauschen
switch

was
which

ganz
completely

einfach
simply

ist
is

dafür
for this

brauchen
need, require

Sie
you, *formal*

nur
only

an
a

die
the

Reling
deckrail

zu
to

stehen
Stand

Wer
Who

auch
ever

immer
always

sich
himself

für
for

einen	a
Untergang	Sinking
im	within
Hafen	harbour, port
entscheidet,	decides,
hat	has
zahlreiche	numerous
Vorbereitungen	preparations
zu	to
überwachen	surveil, control
Ein	A, an
Eisberg	Iceberg
muss	must
hergebracht	to be brought here
werden	become
der	which
über	over
Jahre	years
an	at, a
Bord	board
schmilzt	melts
und	and
elektrische	electric
Kontakte	contacts
korrodieren	corrode
lässt	lets
Die	The
Bordbar	bordbar
muss	must
leergetrunken	be drunk empty
und	and
mehrmals	multiple times
über	over
die	the
Reling	deckrail
erbrochen	vomited
werden	become
Sobald	as soon as
das	the
Navigationsbesteck	navigation toolkit
zum	to
Erlegen	to bag, *kill*
eines	of a
Hirsches	deer, adult male
der	of the
am	at
neu	new
entstandenen	appeared
Schiffswald	ships forest
per	through, via, per
Schnellevolution	fast track evolution
entstand	evovlved
umgewidmet	rededicate, repurpose
werden	become
konnte	could, *past*
kann	can
der	the
Untergang	sinking
beginnen	begin
allerdings	but, though

ist is	**sodass** such that	**ist** is
die the	**das** the	**kann** can
Umwidmung rededication	**Schiff** ship	**dann** then
von of	**fünfzig** fifty	**der** the
Navigationsbesteck navigation toolkit	**Seemeilen** sea miles	**Untergang** sinking
nur only	**fernab** apart of, (far) away	**beginnen** begin
auf on	**aller** of all	**Die** The
hoher high	**Länder** countries	**MS** ms
See sea	**ankert** anchors	**daneben** \splash/
zulässig Admissible, permissible	**Dann** Then	**aber** but
Also Thus	**wird** will be	**wäre** was, would be
muss must	**das** the	**nicht** not
der the	**Navigationsbesteck** navigation toolkit	**die** the
Hafen harbour, port	**umgewidmet.** rededicated	**MS** ms
überflutet overflooded	**Sobald** As soon as	**daneben** beside!
werden become	**der** the	**wenn** if
sowie as well as	**Hirsch** deer, male, adult	**sie** they
angrenzende adjacent, bordering	**noch** yet	**nicht** not
Landflächen land areas	**nicht** not	**spontan** spontaneously
	weggeschwommen swam away	**Landmassen** land masses

aufschütten to bank up	**Sand** sand	**ersetzt** replaced
könnte could, *subj.*	**in** in	**und** anf
auf on	**jeder** every	**per** per
denen which	**Kajüte** cabin	**Polonaise** polonaise
ein a	**direkt** directly	**zu** to
Naturschutzgebiet protective area	**hinter** behind	**einem** a
ausgelobt dedicated: *offered, advertised, ,ritually'*	**der** which	**Förderband** conveyor belt
werden are being, become	**Türe** door	**geschafft** carried (*not done, created*)
kann can	**im** in the	**worauf** upon which
wohin ~ where at	**Teppich** carpet	**der** the
der the	**sowie** as well as, just like	**Sand** sand
Hirsch deer, *male, adult*	**als** as	**eingelagert** stored *into*
fliehen flee	**Matratzenfüllung** matress stuffing	**wird** is
darf may	**Der** The	**bis** until
Dafür Therefore	**Sand** sand	**eine** a
lagert stores	**wird** is being	**steife** stiff
die the	**gesammelt** collected	**Brise** breeze, *wind, air, soft*
MS ms	**mit** with	**ihn** him
daneben besides	**getrocknetem** dried	**von** off
	Salzwassersalz salt made of salt water	**Deck** deck

bläst blows	**Hafenrundfahrten** harbour round tours	**Bord** board
bis until	**können** can	**dabei** while
zum to	**keine** no	**helfen** help
Grund ground	**gebucht** booked, ordered	**die** the
aufschüttet to pile-tip a heap	**werden** be, become	**Gegend** area
und and	**außer** except	**zu** to
so thus	**Sie** you, *formal*	**erkunden** discover
eine a	**bringen** bring	**und** and
natürliche natural	**ein** a	**seine** his
Landmasse land mass	**Schlauchboot** rubber boat	**Gedanken** thoughts
errichtet Construct, erect, set up	**mit** with	**anhören**, hear, to listen to, ~ *ahear* ~
Optional optional, *fakultativ*	**einem** a	**während** while
helfen help	**Außenbordmotor** outboard motor	**Sie** you, *formal*
Asteroiden asteroids	**mit** with	**in** in
und and	**dann** then	**Ihrem** their
Vulkanausbrüche volcanic eruptions	**dürfen** may	**Schiff** ship
bei at, with, during, intendinglyly	**Sie** you, *formal*	**warten** wait
der the	**dem** the	**Eine** A, an
Landgewinnung. ~ land gain	**Entertainer** entertainer	**Audienz** audience
	an at	**auf** on

Hafenwasser
harbour water

zwar
rightly so

aber
but

immerhin
at least

auch
as well

auf
on

Ihre
you, *formal*

Kosten
cost, expense

Das
The

ist
is

insofern
insofar, in this respect

okay
okay

als
as

dass
that

Sie
you, *formal*

hernach
afterwards

zu
to

einem
a

auf
on

den
the

Kopf
head

gestellten
stood, placed

Kirchenschiff
church ship, nave

zurückkehren
return

Vierte
fourth

Zäsur
caesur

Es
It

sind
are

mehrere
multiple

Schiffe
ships

die
which

sind
are

aber
but, though

verschieden
different

orientiert
orientated

Nur
Only

manche
some

fliegen
fly

stur
stubborn

gen'
in direction of

Himmel
sky

Jeder
Every

Versuch
Attempt

wird
is

anstandslos
~ without objection, doubt

durchgeführt
conducted, processed,
guided through

und
and

als
as

Erfolg
success

verbucht,
marked up, noted

insbesondere
especially

die
the

Inneneinrichtung
interior furnishing

der
of the

Reling
deck rail

betreffend
concerning

Nun
Now, *well,*

da
as

man
one

an
at

der
the

Reling
deckrail

stehend
standingly

auch
as well

von
off

Deck
deck

blicken
look, regard

kann
can

in
in

Richtung
direction

Hafengelände
harbour area

oder
or

zur
to the

Brücke
bridge

und
and

zum
to the, direction

Kabinenaufbau
cabin construction

für
for

die
the

luxuriösen
luxurious

Suiten
suites

und
and

Restaurants
restaurants

vermisse
miss, *a person*

ich
I

die
the, *female*

Fähre
ferry

zwischen
between

den
the

beiden
two, both

Sprungbrettern
spring board, diving board

im
in the

Pool
pool

„Wassernass",
"Waterwet",

der
which

auch
also

an
at

der
the

Reling
deck rail

mit
with

seinem
his

Namen
name

ausgeschildert
signs, direction signs were provided

wird
is being

Und
And

da
there

wird
is

man
one

sich
oneself

als
as

aufmerksamer
attentive

Fahrgast
passenger

gerne
gladly, willingly

daran
at [this]

erinnern
remind

lassen
to let, *to allow and expect to be reminded*

wo
where

der
the

Pool
pool

ist
is

nur
only

leider
unfortunately

achtete
respected, paid attention

man
one

darauf
at [it]

stets
constantly, always. continually, throughout

in
in

die
the

falsche
wrong

Richtung
direction

auszuschildern
to put, provide signs, to signpost

Deshalb
Therefore

landen
land, arrive

viele
many

mit
with

ihrem
their

Handtuch
towel

im
in the

Maschinenraum
engine room, machine room

Und
And

da
there

kann
can

man
one

höchstens
at most

mit
with

anpacken
to launch into, to tackle along: *mit anpacken*

Eine
One, A

metallische
metallic

Reling
deck rail

ist
is

ganz
completely

schnell
quickly, swift

beschrieben:
described

Sie
She, it

verhindert
hinders, avoids, pre-empts

dass
that

Menschen
humans, humen

die
the

Laufffläche
boardwalk, walking area, surface

oberhalb
above

des
the, *genitiv*

Schwimmkörpers
floating body

verlassen
leave

können
can, are able to

oder
or

müssen
have to, must

Bevor
before, *time*

aber
but, though

der
the

nächste
next

Präsenztermin
„presence appointment"

über
above, *concerning [topic]*

die
the

online-Option
online-option

des
of the

Sektglases
sparking wine glass

der
of the

fremden
strange

Frau
woman

erfolgt
takes place

muss
must

der
the

Fahrgast
passenger

an
at

der
the

Reling
deckrail

ein
a

älterer
elderly

Herr
Mister

mittleren
of middle

Alters
age

der
who

jung
young

ist
is

wie
like

ein
a

Achtzehnjähriger
eightteen year old

komplexe
complex

Aufgaben
tasks, challenges

an
at

einem
a

Wecker
reveil, *french*, alarm clock

lösen
solve

damit
such that

er
he

ihn
him

nicht
not

wieder
again

abstellen
to turn off

kann
can

Hier
Here

an
at

der
the

Reling
deckrail

ist
is

immer
always

Bewegung
movement

entweder
either

es
it

passiert
passes, happens

nichts
nothing

was
which

völlig
completely, "fully"

neu
new

ist
is

in
in

der
the

Ideengeschichte
history of ideas

unseres
of our

Planeten
planet

oder
or

aber
though, but

es
it

wird
is

eine
a

Kreuzfahrt
cruise

vorbereitet.
prepared

Denn
For, reason

auf
on

eine
a

Kreuzfahrt
cruise

folgt
follows

stets
steadily, constantly,
expecteably

eine
a

neue
new

Kreuzfahrt
cruise

Und
And

da
as, *there*

wird
is being

dann
then, *consecutive*

natürlich
naturally, of course

auch
also

mit
with

Trumpf
trump

und
and

Joker
joker

um
for, (around)

Geld
money

gespielt
played

Die
The

Seekrankheit
seasickness

an
at

der
the

Reling
deckrail

hängt
depends

vom
on

Seegang
sea condition

ab
de (depends, abhängen)

anders
different

als
to

auf
on

der
the

Brücke
bridge

oder
or

im
in the

Maschinenraum
machine room

wo
where

sie
they

vom
of the

Maschinenraum
machine room

beziehungsweise
respectively

der
the

Brücke
bridge

und
and

von
of

der
the

Sprechverbindung
voice communication

zwischen
between

beiden
both

Räumen
rooms

abhängt
depends.

Die
The

einzigen
only

Wellen
waves

die
which

bei
at

einem
a

angetauten
towed, fixed in a port using ropes

Schiff
ship

relevant
relevant

sind
are

sind
are

solche
such, *those, of such kind*

die
which

die
the

Wasserschutzpolizei
water police

und
and

den
the

Zoll
toll, tax, financial, economical border control

betreffen
concern, relate to, refer

Wird
Is

gegen
against

die
the

Produktion
production

von
of

Holstern
holsters

gestreikt
striked, no work protest

müssen
must

die
the

Beamtinnen
officials, functionaries

ihr
their

Schießeisen
"schootiron", firearm

in
in

Händen
hands

halten
hold

während
while, *during*

Kontrollen
controls

durchgeführt
[are being] conducted

werden
be, become

Das
The

Schiff
ship

sinkt
sinks

spontan
spontaneously

und
and

taucht
"dive up", appear, *dive*

wieder
again

auf [auftauchen]
up [dive]

das
the

Hafenbecken
harbour basin

is
is

tiefer
deeper

als
than, as, *comparison*

der
the

Tiefgang
flotation depth

des
of the, *genitiv*

Schiffs
ship

Wievielte
Howmuchth

Zäsur
Zäsur

Das
The

Mitzählen
to count with, to count along

ist
is

zwar
indeed, right so

gestattet
allowed, authorized

aber
but

es
it

stört
disarranges

beim
during

Nachdenken
to overthink, to think about
something after it happened

Die
The

MS
ms

daneben
not hit

ist
is

ein
a

nasses
wet

Schiff
ship

mit
with

Anker
anchor

das
which

im
in the

Hafen
port, harbour

liegt
lies

und
and

auf
on

eine
a

Ausfahrt
drive

vorbereitet
prepared

wird
is

Die
The

Taue
ropes

liegen
lie, lay down

an
at

den
the

metallischen
metallic

Pylonen
pyloons

spezieller
of special

Form
shape

und
and

bewirken
effect, *verb*

die
the

Stationarität
stationarity

des
of the

Schiffs
ship

die
which

leicht
easily

aufgehoben
canceled, suspended

werden
to become

kann
can

indem
by, in, through

die
the

Taue
big ship-ropes

recycelt
recyceled

werden
to become

Dafür
Therefore

werden
are being

sie
they

von
of

einer
a

Vertreterin
representant

der
ot the

Reederei
shipping company

als
as

abgeschrieben
~ amortised, *regarding taxes*

definiert
defined

von
of

einer
a

Fachkraft
special worker

für
for, of

12 - 13

Recycling
recycling

als
as

Wertstoff
valueable material

deklariert
declared

und
and

von
of, by, from

einer
a

Firma
enterprise, company

für
for

**Vertäuungsgegenstandproduk
tion**
production of items to fix
ships in a port with

in
in

situ
place, latin

herbeigezaubert.
to magiced to place

Dadurch
Through this, Thus

konnten
could

die
the

Kosten
costs, expenses

für's
for

Vertäuen
fixing a ship with big ropes

und
and

Ablegen
the process of departing with
a ship

drastisch
drastically

gesenkt
lowered, decreased

werden
be, become

Solche
Of such kind

Vorgänge
Processes

werden
are being

permanent
permanently

der
the, to the

MS
MS

daneben
besides

angelastet,
charged to, accused to

aber
but

dennoch
however

von
of

anderen
other

Reedereien
shipowning company

imitiert
imitated

Es
It

ist
is

nicht
not

möglich
possible

sich
oneself

bezüglich
concerning, relating to

der
the

Frage
question

nach
about, of

dem
the

Borden
boarding, entering a ship

an
at

Flughäfen
airport

zu
to

orientieren
orientate.

Formalitätisch
regarding formalities,
neologism

schon
already, indeed

klar
clear

aber
but

die
the

anfahrbare
enables, allows to drive to

Treppe
stair

ist
is

sowohl
as well as, both, ..

am
at the

Flughafen
airport

als
as well as, and

auch
also

hier
here

im
in the

Hochseehafen
high sea port

nicht
not

für
for

Esel
donkey

geeignet,
suiteable, adequate

was
which

aber
but

nur
only

an
at

Hochseehäfen
high sea ports

per
using, *latin*

Beschilderung
signing, signs, signpostings

angezeigt
displayed, indicated

wird
is to be is like that

Der
The

durchgestrichene
crossed, with a line

Esel
donkey, esel

wird
is

begleitet
accompaigned

von
by

einer
a

Sprechblase
balloon, speech bubble

des
of the

Inhalts
content

„An
"At

der
the

Reling
deck rail

bitte
please

nicht
not

anlehnen,
to lean to
ok
ok

bro?!"
Bru[der]?!"

Das
The

Grau
grey

des
of the

Esels
donkey

orientiert
orientates

sich
itself

dabei
during names circumstance

weniger
less

am
at the

typischen
typiccal

Straßenbelag
street covering

als
than

an
at

der
the

Farbe
color

des
of the

Mondes
moon

wenn
if

der
he

zu
to, for, in value of

circa
around

einem
a

Drittel
third

sichtbar
visible

ist
is

und
and

hoch
high

über
above

dem
the

Gestirn
celestial, heavenly body

steht.
stands

Hier
Here

an
at

der
the

Reling
deck rail

wird
is being

manchmal
sometimes

gestrichen
painted

dabei
during which, while

werden
are being

alle
all

metallischen
metallic

Teile
parts

der
of the

Reling
deck rail

mit
with

Hilfe
help

von
of

Farbe
color

geschönt,
made more beautiful,
enbeautifulled

aber
but

nicht
not

ohne
without

Farbfächer
colour palette

der
which

im
inside

Rettungsring
lifebelt

liegt
lies, to lie, Position

wie
how

ein
a

Abiturient
high school graduate

in
in

seiner
his

Hängematte
hammock

würden
would

Sie
you, *formal*

sich
yourself

einen
a

Livestream
livestream

ansehen
look, watch

in
in

dem
which

ein
a

Abiturient
high-school graduate

oder
or

gar
even, evenmore

eine
a

Abiturientin
high-school graduate, female

in
in

einer
a

Hängematte
hammock

liegt?
lies

Die
The

Reling
deck rail

ist
is

der
the

einzige
only

Ort
place

an
on

Bord
board

an
at

dem
which

man
one

sich
oneself

wirklich
really

ruhig
silently

aufhalten
linger, remain, stay

kann
can

neben
besides

dem
the

Krankenzimmer
sickroom

dem
the

Kühlhaus
cold storage house

für
for

Verstorbene,
passed away ones

der
the

Bordbank
board bank

und
and

im
in the

Maschinenraum
engine room

natürlich
of course

Auch
As well as

im
in the

Restaurant
restaurant

am
at the

Tisch
table

des
of the

Kapitäns
captain

geht
goes, passes, 'happens'

es
it

meist
mostly

ruhig
silently

zu
>> *etwas*, something, *geht zu*,
happens

wenn
if

nicht
not

gerade
just, timely

ein
a

Oligarch
oligarch

mit
with

einem
a

Kapitalisten
capitalist

streitet
argue, fight

wobei
whereat

der
the

Kapitän
captain

der
the

Kapitalist
capitalist

ist
is

und
and

der
the

Oligarch
oligarch

der
the

Kapitän
captain

werden
to become

will
wants

Deshalb
Therefor

muss
has to, must, is obliged to

man
one

einen
a

ruhigen
silent

Platz
place

stets
constantly, always

genießen
enjoy

solange
as long as

das
this

möglich
possible
ist.
is

Die
The

Reling
deckrail

ist
is

ein
a

ruhiger
silent

Ort
place

mit
with

vielen
a lot of, many

Möglichkeiten
possibilities

Beispielsweise
For example

kann
can

man
one

sich
oneself

mithilfe
with the help of, using

der
the

Reling
deck rail

an
at

der
the

Reling
deck rail
festhalten,
to hang on, grip

genaugenommen
strictly speaking, in the strict sense

ist
is

aber
but, however, though

auch
as well, too, also

das
this

nicht
not

gestattet
allowed, authorized

siehe
watch

weiter
further

vorn
in the front of; more near at the beginning

im
in the

Text
text

„An
»At

der
the

Reling
deck rail

bitte
please

nicht
not

anlehnen,
to lean on, hang on

ok?".
ok?«

Die
The

Bordbibliothek
ships library

enthält
contains

blaue
blue

Bücher
books

und
and

solche
such

die
that

Seefahrtabenteuer
adventures of the sea

thematisieren
thematize, contain

Das
This

begeistert
thrills

nicht
not

nur
only

FarbenthusiastInnen
color enthusiasts

sondern
but

auch
also

den
the

kleinen
small
sturen
stubborn, partially positive

Franzosen
french man

der
who

stets
usually, constantly

darin
within

weilt
to remain, stay

und
and

sich
himself

der
the

geselligen
convival, sociable

Ruhe
silence

erfreut
pleased

Man
Man

erkennt
recognizes

ihn
him

an
at, using, via, through

der
the

Trikolore
french flag tricolore, three colors

mit
with

der
which

er
he

sich
himself

eine
a

Wunde
wound

an
at

der
the

linken
left

Faust
fist

verband
dressed, *med.*

die
which

entstand
emerged

als
when

er
he

wegen
because of, ~*through*

eines
a

versehentlich
accidentially

liegengelassenen
let lie

roten
red

Buches
book
die
the

Sicherheitsscheibe
safety shoes

des
of the

Feueralarms
fire alarm

einschlug
punched, stroke

In
In

der
the

Bibliothek
library

gefangen
catched, trapped

schaffte
to make, achieve something;
also: created

er
he

es
it

nie
never

in
in

den
the

Ambulanzbereich
ambulance area

des
of the

lateinischen
latin

mächtig
mighty, regarding languages:
to be able to use a language

wäre
would

es
it

für
for

ihn
him

auch
also, as well

nicht
not

möglich
possible

gewesen
has been

dort
there

hinzugelangen
get to arrive somewhere

Ein
A

Matrose
sailor

stellte
placed, put, set

einmal
once

die
the

Vermutung
hypothese, assumption

an
>> ~ to set up a hypothesis

dass
that

so
thus

der
the

rote
red

Teil
part

der
of the

Trikolore
tricolore

entstand
evolved

dass
that

nämlich
namely, that is to say

das
that

blauweiße
blue-white

Taschentuch
tissue

mit
with

Blut
blood

getränkt
saturated, soaked

eben
eben, just, such, then, just now

sich
itself
verfärbte
(en)coloured

im
in the, using

Eilverfahren
fast process, fast lane

vom
of the

französischen
french
Konsulat
consulate

an
a, on, at

Bord
board

zur
to the, as

Trikolore
tricolore

geweiht
sanctified, dedicated

ist
is

nun
now

eben
even, just now, ~ *nivellating emotions*

die
the

Trikolore
tricolore

Bestandteil
component

der
of the

Bordbibliothek:
board library, ships library

"ich
„I

kann
can

sie
her

nicht
not

vermissen",
miss, a person

sagt
says

der
the

unfreiwillige
unvolontary

Bibliothekar
librarian

und
and

legt
lays

dem
the

Mann
man

an
at

der
the

Reling
deck rail

ein
a

Buch
book

in
in

die
the

Hand
hand

das
which

dieser
this, he

versehentlich
accidentally

über
over
Bord
board

wirft
throws

und
and

einfach
simply, easily

fallen
drop

lässt
let

Die
The

Buchstaben
characters

purzeln
tumble

aus
out

den
the

Seiten
pages

verteilen
spread

sich
themselves

ein
a

bisschen little	**herbeigeschafft** carried to place	**Pool** pool
wie like	**als** as	**auch** also, too
Schrot buckshot, lead shot	**Werk** work	**um** such that
über above	**des** of the	**sich** himself
dem the	**Teufels** devil	**wegen** because of
Wasser water	**verunglimpft** denigrated, denounced	**der** the
in in	**und** and	**aufwändigen** laborious
das which	**der** the	**Suche** Searching
auch as well, too	**Autor** author	**abzukühlen** chilling
das the	**gesucht** looked for	**200** 200
sie they	**verhaftet** arrested	**Schritte** steps
getragen carried	**und** and	**erlaubt** allows
habende having	**zum** to the	**er** he
Papier paper	**Poolreinigungsservice** pool cleaning service	**sich** himself
hineinplumpst plump into	**abkommandiert** assigned	**noch** still, if anything
Eilig speedy, urgent, hastily	**Seither** since	**pro** per
wird is being	**sucht** looks for	**Stunde** hour
ein a	**der** the	**mehr** more
neues new	**Autor** author	**würden** would
Buch book	**den** the	**zu** to

Überhitzung
overheating

führen
lead

und
and

irgendwer
someone
muss
has to, must

ja
yes, *(veiling the circumstances)*

das
the

Sieb
sieve, mesh, filter

am
at the

Pool
pool

den
the

Pool
pool

und
and

die
the

Umgebung
environment; rather the surrounding area

des
of the

Pools
pool

reinigen
clean

Die
The

im
in the

britischen
british

Englisch
english

auch
also, as well, by the way

„Spektakel"
spectacles

genannten
named

Brillen
glasses

der
of the

Fahrgäste
passengers

werden
are being

zu
to, at

Beginn
beginning

der
of the

Fahrt
cruise, drive

konfisziert
confiscated

und
and

während
during

der
the

Fahrt
drive, cruise

wieder
again, "re-"

versteigert
auctionned

So
thus

wird
is being

der
the
Umsatz
turnover

des
of the

bordeigenen
bord-own, on board

Optikers
optician

erhöht
raised

„Sie
You, formal

wünschen
wish

eine
a, an

Anpassung
adaption

der
of the

Seestärke?
ayesight?, properly »Sehstärke« with sea/See and Seh-/sight-

Kein
No

Problem
Problem

Dürfte
may

ich
I

auch

also, as well

das
the

Gestell
rack, frame

an
at

Ihre
her

Bedürfnisse
needs, requirements,
necessities

anpassen?".
adapt?«

Die
The

Malereien
Paintings

die
which

die
the

einfarbig
monochrome, one coloured

gestrichenen
coated, painted

Bordwände
vessel's side, shell plate

überdecken
cover

dienen
serve

bei
during

Anlandungen
disembarkments

an
at

die

the

Museumsinsel
museum island

als
as

Camouflage.
camouflage

Aber
But

das
the

Schiff
ship

liegt
lies

hier
here

im
in

Hafen
harbour

es
it

läuft
walks, runs

nicht
not

aus,
out

da
because

es
it

von
of

innen
inside

her

to here

dicht
tight, dense

ist
is

und
and

bedarf
requires
einzig
solely

des
(of) the

Segens
blessings

eines
of a

Geistlichen,
spiritual, reverend, cleric

der
who

an
a, at

Bord
board

eine
a

eigene
own

Kapelle
chapel

unterhält
maintain, support, keep

Wer
Who

die
the

Kapelle
chapel

betritt

make a step into

läuft
runs

Gefahr
danger

von
of

maskierten
masked

TäterInnen,
offenders, wrongdoers,
gendered

die
who

beständig
steadily

Tabak
tabacco

rauchen
smoke, verb

überwältigt
to bear down

zu
to

Boden
ground

gedrückt
pushed

und
and

zwangsgeimpft
forcibly vaccinated

oder
or

anderweitig
otherwise

gekränkt
sickened

zu

to

werden.
be

Zweiundzwanzig
twentytwo

Mal
times

wird
is being

pro
per

Tag
day

die
the

heilige
holy

Messe
mess

gefeiert:
celebrated

Das
The

einzige
only

Geräusch
sound

das
which, that

den
the

Aufenthalt
presence, stay, residence,
habitation

an
a

Bord
board

verunbequemlicht,

make non comfortable,
neologism

ist
is

das
the

Quietschen
squeaking

der
of the

Reifen
tires

bei
at

der
the

Abfahrt
departure.

Pontons
Pontoons

befinden
find themselves, are, are
stored

sich
themselves

unter
under

Deck
deck

auf
on

Ebene
level

2,
two

achtern
aft, back of the ship

man
one

muss

has to, must

den
the

Steuerbord-Flur
bow side-, starboard-corridor,
hallway

entlanggehen
to walk along

bis
until

zu
>until, to

einem
a

Raum
room

in
in

dem
which

Pontons
Pontoons

schon
already

beim
during

Bau
construction

des
of the

Schiffs
ship

eingelagert
stored

wurden
were

weil
because

sie

they

weder
nor

durch
through

die
the

Flure
floors

noch
nor

durch
through

die
the

Treppenhäuser
staircases, stairways

passen
match

Sechste
sixth

Zäsur
censorship

Pontons
Pontoons

sind
are

relevant
relevant

für
for

Schiffe
ships

und
and

für
for

Kreuzfahrten
cruises

Oft
Often

ist
are

die
the

Reling
deck rail

daran
at this

interessiert
interested

mehrere
multiple

Sinneskanäle
sense channels

anzusprechen
to speak to, to start a chat

einige
some

Matrosen
sailors

aber
but, contradictingly

haben
have

sich
themselves

daran
at, at this

gewöhnt,
get used to, accustom

die
the

Reling
deck rail

zu
to

filmen
film, *verb*

zu
to

beobachten
observe, watch

oder
or

Pläne
plans

für
for

eine
a

Verwendung
use

nach
after

ihrem
their

Ableben
"Offliving"

anzustellen
hypothezise, to put into place

Beispielsweise
As an example

wird
is being

der
the

Bau
Building, constructing

von
of

Panzern
tanks

antizipiert
anticipated

oder
or

aber
but, as well

sogar
even

ein
a

neuer
new

Anker
anchor

in
in

Form
shape

einer
of a

großen
big

Reisschüssel
rice bowl

und
and

der
the

Bau
construction

von
of

Umkleidekabinen
changing rooms

vorgesehen,
stipulated, envisaged, scheduled

die
the

an
a

Stelle
place

der
the

Rettungsschiffe
lifeboat, emergency boat, ship

angebracht
attatched

werden
are, are being

Überwachung
Surveillance

findet
takes, *"finds"*

hier
here

an
at

der
the

Reling
deck rail

insofern
insofar

nicht
not

statt, *stattfinden*
place, *to take place, happen*

als
as

dass
that

die
the

Matrosen,
sailors

vor
before

allem
every; "vor allem":especially

jene,
those

die
who

der
the

Vereingung
Union

„Junge
"Young

Nutzmetapher"
Utility metaphore"

angehören
belong to, *passive*

einfach
easily

die
the

Gewohnheiten
habits

der
of the

Vereinigung
unification

„alte
old

Nutzmetapher"
utility metaohore"

übernommen
overtake, "inherit", adapt

und
and

rechtfertigt
justify

haben
have

Deshalb
Therefor

findet
finds

die
the

Überwachung
surveillance

von
of

anderen
other

Häfen
harbours

aus
from; "von .. aus" from from somewhere else

statt
place

in
in

denen
which

sich
themselves

„geile
wicked, horny, lustful

Nutzmetapher"-
Utility metaphore

und
and

„nachdenkliche
overthinking

Nutzmetapher"-Vereinigungen
utility metaphore

unterschiedlichster
of the most vorying variety of; of most different kind; of widest spectre

Namen
names

herausbildeten
emerge

Das
The

geschäftige
busy

Treiben
floating, drifting

an
on

Bord
board

eines
of a

Schiffes
ship

kann
can

nirgends
nowhere

besser
better

beobachtet
observed

werden
be, being

als
as

an
at

der
the

Reling
deck rail

ist
Is

die
the

Reling
deck rail

mit
with

vielen
many

Menschen
humans

bestückt
~enpieced, populated,
'equipped'

kann
can

auf
~upon, on top of

eine
a

gute
good

Witterung
weather, weathering, scent

geschlussfolgert
concluded

werden
be, being

ist
is

sie
she

aber
but

Seelen-leer
soul-empty

liegt
lies

entweder
either

ein
a

notwendiger
necessary

Landgang
shore leave, "landwalk"

vor
'in front of'

oder
or

aber
but

es
it

regnet
rains

stark
strongly

bei
during, *also: near*

Kälte
cold, noun

und
and

diesem
this, that

was
what

„Wellengang"
'sea swell', "wavewalk"

genannt
called, named

wird
~ is being

Ein
A

Schiffsdeck
ships deck

ist
is

niemals
never

deshalb
because, for, indicating a
reason

leer
empty

weil
because

das
the

Schiff
ship

Pause
pause

macht
makes, *(pauses)*

Entweder
Either

die
the

Reederei
ship owning company

tauscht
(ex-)changes

das
the

Personal
personnel, staff, (crew)

aus
"ex-" of 'exchanges'

oder
or

das
the

Schiff
ship

ist
is

In
in

einem
a

Dock
dock

Untergänge
Sinkings

finden
find, *here: part of 'take place'*

nicht
not

statt
'place'

Außer
Except

im
in

Hafen
port, harbour

Siebente
seventh

Zäsur
turning point

Das
The

Untergehen
Sinking

ist
is

Schiffen
ships

nicht
not

untersagbar
'interdicteable', forbiddeable,
prohibideable

Seit
Since

kurzem
short, timely

bin
am

ich
I

fast
almost

ein
a

Mitglied
member

von
of

der
the

einzigen
only

Partei,
Partei (group of seriously
celebrating politicians)

deren
whose

Name
name

auch
also, too

für
for

Kinder
kids

verständlich
understandeable

ist
is

Da
There

ist
is

zwar
(indeed), indicating a fact to
take account of

schlimm
bad, severe

aber
but

egal
equal, howeverly

weil
because

das
the

nahezu
almost

tatsächliche
actual

eben
even

nur
only

nicht
not

und
and

nicht
not

fatalerweise
fatally

nicht
not

zutrifft
applies

Die
The

Entscheidung
decision

der
the

einzigen
only

Partei
Partei

beizutreten
join

deren
whose

Name
name

mir
mee

einleuchtete
make sense to someone

dauerte
lastet, timely

fast
almost

mein
my

ganzes
entire

Leben
life

Die
The

selbstverfreilich
~self-evident

alkoholfreien
alcohol-free

Alkoholmischgetränke
alcohol-mix-drinks

die
which

fremden
strange

beeindruckten
impressed

Personen
persons

der
the

alte
old

Chemiker
chemician

der
who

mir
me

von
of

seinem
his

Tanz
dance

mit
with

den
the

Behörden
institutions

erzählte
told

der
who

aber
but

eigentlich
actually

ein
a

Kampf
fight

war
was

und
and

nicht
not

lachen
laugh

wollte
wanted

Der
The

komplette
complete

Rücken
back

war
was

voller
full of

Schrammen
scratches

die
which

mit
with

einer
a

Zahl
number

verknüpft
interconnected, linked,
connected

wurden
were

Achtzehn
Eightteen

das
the

Bild
image

des
of the

völlig
fully

eingekerkerten
incarcerated

ausgeschlossenen
excluded

aber
but

mit
with

einem
a

selbstherrlichen
egomaniacal

Sinn
Sense

versehenen
supplied, provided, endowed,
endowed

Zweck
purpose

bedachten,
concerned, considered,
pondered ~~

für
for

jenen
thees

niemals
neverly

verständlichen
understandeable

Zweck
purpose

hat
has

bereits
already

sein
his

möglichstes
most possible

getan
done

nämlich
namely

für
for

sich
himself

selbst
self

gesorgt
cared

Die
The

Eigenheit
~pecularity, regarding a characteristic

sich
himself

zu
to

seinesgleichen
ones of own kind

zu
to

gesellen
consort, join

war
was

nämlich
namely, actually

vor
before

der
the

Industrialisierung
industrialization

gesellschaftlich
concerning the society

akzeptierter
accepteable

Konsens
consensus

der
which

von
from

der
the

nun
now

folgenden
following

Geschichte
history

abgelöst
~replaced, (without negativity)

wurde
was

„**Meine**
My

Knochen
bones

sind
are

mürbe
~mürbe

von
of

der
the

Ausbeutung
exploition

die
which

mein
my

Körper
body, *alive*

erfährt
experiences

und
and

von
of

den
the

Angriffen
attacks

die
which

er
he

abwehren
repel

will
wants

und
and

von
of

den
the

Opferungen
Sacrifications

die
which

man
one

sich
oneself

auf
on

beiden
both

Seiten
sides

des
of the

Flusses
river

zugestehen
admit, allow

will"
want.«

Solange
As long as

aber
but

an
at

der
the

Reling
deck rail

ein
a

Platz
place

für
for

mich
me

ist,
is,

werde
will

ich
I

diesen
that one

nicht
not

preisgeben
abandon, give up, surrender

Im
In the

Gegenteil
opposite (contrarily)

„die
„the

Errungenschaften
achievements

der
of the

Sozialdemokratie
social democracy

gelten
count, are valid

an
at, on

wie
just like, like

unter
under

Deck
deck

gleich
equally

nur
only

ist
is

die
the

Frage
question

ob
whether

man
one

von
from

außerhalb
outside

der
the

Metapher
metaphore

davon
of it

Gebrauch
use

machen
make

darf
may

und
and

kann
can

von
of

immenser
immens

Bedeutung
importance, significance, meaning

für
for

den
the

Spießer
~ Babbit, burgeois, square

an
on

Deck
deck

sein",
be"

sagte
said

ein
a

Reiseführer
travel guide

der	**mit**	**also**
who	with	thus, then (conclusive)
eine	**einem**	**hatte**
a	a	had
tschechische	**irischen**	**ich**
czech	irish	I
eine	**Reiseführer**	**Schmerzen**
a	travel guid	pain
russische	**der**	**weil**
russian	who	because
eine	**sich**	**ich**
a	himself	I
österreichische	**selbst**	**mich**
austrian	self	myself
eine	**über**	**körperlich**
a	over	physically
frankophone	**das**	**überlegenen**
francophone	the	superior
und	**Deck**	**Personen**
and	deck	persons
eine	**führte**	**mit**
a	guided	with
britische	**und**	**großen**
british	and	big
Reisegruppe	**anderen**	**brummenden**
travel group	others	humming, buzzing, grumbling
über	**davon**	**Waffen**
over	of it, of that	weapons
das	**über**	**beugen**
the	about	bow, verb
Kreuzfahrtschiff	**sein**	**musste**
cruise ship	his	had to, musted
führte	**internetfähiges**	**die**
led, lead	internet-capable	the, which
Er	**Sektglas**	**mich**
He	sparkling wine glass	me
kollidierte	**berichtete**	**weder**
collided	reported	nor
	Überall	**über**
	Everywhere	about

ihre
their

Pläne
plans

informierten
informed

also
thus

auch
as well

mich
myself

zwangen
forced

sie
they

beherrschen
rule, reign

zu
to

wollen
want

„Wann
"When

immer
ever

Sie
she

einen
a

Plan
plan

haben
have

müssen
must

Sie
you, formal

diesen
this (special) one

an
at

Bord
board

und
and

abseits
offsite, aside

von
of, by

an
a, at

Bord
board

eines
of a

Kreuzfahrtschiffes
cruise ship

aussprechen
to speak out

und
and

werden
are being

das
that, this

auch
also, correspondingly

tun.",
do

sagte
said

der
the

irische
irish

Reiseleiter
travel guid

zu
to

einem
a

amerikanischen
american

Unternehmensberater
consultant, business consultant

den
which

er
he

über
over

sein
his

Armband
bracelet

auf's
on the

Ohr
ear

geschaltet
switched, in the sense of 'connected'

hatte
got, received

Aber
But

das
that

lenkt
distracts

alles
everything

nur
only

ab
"dis-"-tracts

von
of

der
the

Perpsektive
perspective

die
which

man
one

nur
only

von
of

der
the

Reling
deck rail

eines
of a

Schiffes
ship

aus
from

genießen
enjoy

kann
can

„Ohne
"Without

Sektglas
sparkling wine glass

aufzuwachsen
to 'to grow up'

war
was

schwer
hard

für
for

mich
me

also
as well, too

antizipierte
anticipated

ich
I

das
the

Verhalten
behaviour

anderer
of others

und
and

beschuldigte
blamed

sie
them

meiner
of my

paranoiden
paranoid

Ängste
fears

um
in order to

derer
relating to the previously considered object

mithilfe
with the help of

meiner
my

beiden
both

Richtungen
directions

„Back-"
"Back-

und
and

„Steuerbord"
starboard

zuhause
at home

habhaft
~ to receive ownership, to have, to obtain

zu
to

werden.",
to become, from 'to be'

erläuterte
eludicate, explicate, not 'explain'

der
the

irische
irish

Reiseleiter
travel guide

über
over

eine
a

Lautsprecheranlage
soundspeaker system

weiter
further

die
which

aber
but

plötzlich
suddenly

ausfiel
failed, broke down

„Einen
"One

habe
have

ich
I

kopfüber
headfirst

in
in

einen
a

Topf
pot

voll
full of

Geld
money

stecken
stick, put, plug into

lassen
let

der
which

vom
of the

bayerischen
bavarian

Landratsamt
district office

Nordschlesien
northern silesia

beständig
steadily

mit
with

Schwarzgeld
black money

und
and

Münzen
coins

gefüllt
filled

wird
is

Ein
A

weiterer
further

muss
must, has to, has to be, become

in
in

der
the

letzten
last

verbliebenen
remaining

Monarchie
monarchy

auf
on

diesem
this

Planeten
planet

Longdrinks
long drinks

mischen
mix

und
and

ein
a

weiterer
further, "an additional one"

baut
builds, constructs

antriebslose
driveless, motorless

autonome
autonomous

Maschinen
machines

ohne
without

Steuereinheit
steering unit

in
in

der
the

sächsischen
saxon

Schweiz
switzerland

Von
Out of, from

dort
there

aus
out, out of there, from ..

migriert
migrates

jener
this one

regelmäßig
regularily

nach
to

Rumänien
romania

um
for

sich
himself

als
as

neuer
new

Heiland
saviour

vorzustellen
to introduce

und
and

spielt
plays

dann
then

mit
with

Ameisen
ants

am
at the

Strand
beach

fangen.",
catch

ergänzte
added, completed

er
he

durch
through

lautes
loud

Brüllen
roaring

„Der
The

Weisheit
wisdom

letzter
last

Schluss
(con)clusion

der
which

stets
usually, steadily

dem
the

jüngeren
younger

angelastet
blamed to

wird
is

kontextualisiert
contextualizes

man
one

die
the

eigene
own

Konsideration
consideration

bezüglich
regarding

der
the

neu-europäischen
european

Auslegung
interpretation

des
of the

kategorischen
categorical

Imperativs
imperative

ist
is

insofern
insofar

mit
with

einer
a

semipermeablen
semipermeable

Membran
membrane

vergleichbar
comparable

als
as

dass
that

eine
a

einmal
once

geäußerte
expressed, uttered

Tatsache
fact, "deedthing"

nicht
not

mehr
any more

revidiert
revided

werden
are being

kann
can
außer
except

man
one

befindet
finds

sich
oneself

an
at

der
the

Reling
deck rail

oder
or

in
in

einem
a

leeren
empty

Raum
room

mit
with

unendlicher
infinite

Ausdehnung
extention

und
and

immateriellen
immaterial

Grenzen",
borders",

erläuterte
explicated

der
the
irische
irish

Reiseleiter
travel guide

rückwärts
backwards

laufend
walking

einem
to an

arabischen
arabic

Reporter
reporter

japanischer
(of) japanese

und
and

venezuelanischer
(of) venezuelan

Abstammung
origin

„Oh,
"Oh

hi",
hi

sagte
says

er
he

und
and

drehte
turns

sich
himself

um
around

einhundertachtzig
onehundredandeighty

Grad
degrees

nun
now

geraden
straight

Schrittes
steps, noun, pl, "of steps"

hinter
behind

meinem
my

Rücken
back

die
the

Reling
deck rail

entlangflanierend
stroll along

Achte
Eighth

Zäsur
turning point

Rote
Red

Fäden
threads

sind
are

schwer
hard, difficult

zu
to

finden
find

aber
but

immer
always

rot
red

Unendlich
infinitely

komplex
complex

sind
are

bereits
already

die
the

Aufnahmeprüfungen
~assessments, entry,
qualifying examination

zum
to the

Studienfach
field of studies

künstliche
artificial

Mathematik
mathematics

an der
at the

Universität
unifersity

der
of the

unbeliebten
unbeloved

Schulfächer
school subject

in
in

Köln
cologne, not the perfume

Zunächst
at a first glance, not first, but
with high priority, as a first
step of a higher plan

werden
are being

komplexe
complex

Kunstwerke
artworks

geschaffen
created

die
which

es
it

einer
to a

geheimen
secret, veiled

Anzahl
number, amount of

Schiffbrüchiger
ship wrecked

erlaubt
allows, *enables*

zu verstehen
to understand

wie
how

viele
many

Zahlen
numbers

natürlich
natural

sind
are

und
and

wie
how

sie
they

entstehen
evolve, develop, (arise)

Nicht
Not

Babies
Babies

sondern
but

eben
even (a little confusing)

die
the

Peano-Axiome
Peano Axioms

werden
are

in
in

ihrer
their

Entstehung
evolution, development,
arising

analysiert
analyzed

und
and

die
the

eigenen
own

Erfahrungen
experiences

in
in

ein
a

Kunstwerk
artwork

umgesetzt
realized, implemented

das
which

bereits
already

in
in

wenigen
few, small amount

Augenblicken
moments, *blinks of an aye*

nach
after, timely

Auffinden
finding

durch
through

eine
a

dritte
third

Person
person

irrelevant
irrelevant

geworden
were

sein
to be

kann
can

Von
From

Texas
Texas

aus
(to "from") from .. to

starten
start

regelmäßig
regularily

treibstoffbetriebene
fuel-powered

Raketen
rockets

gen
direction, towards

Himmel
sky

jeweils
respectively

mit
with

unterschiedlichem
different

Zweck
purpose

Die
The

MS
MS

daneben
next to it

jedenfalls
at any glance~, anyway, anyhow

die
which

in
in

ihrem
her

Dasein
"Therebeing", *Presence*

von
of, from

einer
a

Pariser
paris

Gynäkologin
gynecologist

gesegnet
blessed

wird
is, constantly

hat
has

insofern
insofar

zweierlei
two of a kind, two, in two aspects

Attribute
attributes

die
which

miteinander
together, jointly

unvereinbar
incompatible, irreconcilable, not fitting

sind
are

als to 'insofar', as	**Sie** You, *formal*	**daneben".** besides
dass that	**bitte** please	**Den** The
die the	**Ihr** your	**Körper** body
örtlichen local	**Gepäck** packaging	**mit** with
Lautsprecherdurchsagen loud speaker announces	**Ihre** Your	**vollem** full
mit with	**Kinder** kids	**Gewicht** weight
denen those	**lassen** let	**an** at
am at the	**wir** we	**die** the
angrenzenden adjacent	**von** of, from	**Reling** deck rail
Bahnhof railway station	**Freiwilligen** voluntaries	**gelehnt** lent, lean
„MS "MS	**die** who	**die** the
daneben" beside"	**mit** with	**ein** one
nur only	**Privilegien** privileges	**früherer** earlier
an at	**betäubt** narcotized, anestethized	**Kapitän** captain
der the	**werden** are	**mit** with
Reling deck rail	**beaufsichtigen** supervisioning	**dem** the
Beachtung consideration, attention	**Ihr** Your	**Protagonisten** protagonist
finden find	**Bahnhof** railway station	**per** per, *using, through*
Beaufsichtigen supervision, imperative	**Hafen** harbour	**Heirat** marriage
	MS MS	**mit** with

dem
the

Schiff
ship

auf
on, for

ewig
ever

verknüpft
linked, associated, connected,
combined

hatte
had

ohne
without

bescheidzusagen
to to tell, to to report

schlief
slept

ich
I

sofort
immediately

ein
in (to sleep in/one)

Neunte
ninth

Zäsur
turning point

Relingen
deck rails

sind
are

nur
only

statisch
statically

stabil
stable

funktional
functionallyly

Achtern
aft

Mitten
in the middle of, *during 12 pm*

am
at the

hell
bright

lichten
bright, light, (Lichtung, a tree-free place in a forest)

Tage
day

ertönte
(en-)sounded

eine
a

Lautsprecherdurchsage
loud speaker announcement

des
of the

vorbeilaufenden
passing

Kapitänes
captain

dass
that

das
the

Auslaufen
departure

kurz
shortly

bevorstehe
impends, soonlies *subjunctive*

In
In

seinem
his

Arm
arm

lag
laid

eine
a

blonde
blonde

Frau
woman

mit
with

rosa
pink

Kleid
robe

das
which

gerade
just

so
just so, tightly, closely; *some opposite of 'almost'*

die
the

Intimsphäre
privacy, intimate sphere

bedeckte
covered

Der
The

Kapitän
captain

ein
a

Mann
man

der
who

seinem
his

Erscheinungsbild
appearance (image)

nach
respectively, regarding, relying to

auf
on

eine
a

Stellenausschreibung
job advertisement

passte
matched

die
the

auf
on

den
the

Kapitän
captain

aus
from

Timothee
"Timothee

und
and

Strumpfl"
sock!"

zugeschnitten
~~ tailored

worden
was

war
was

begleitete
accompaigned

Pfeife
pipe (tobacco-pipe)

rauchend
smokingly

seine
his

Dame
lady

die
who

sich
herself

zwischenzeitlich
meanwhile

in
in

einen
a

Pappaufsteller
paperboard cutout standing thing

mit
with

Verkaufsbotschaft
~ a seller's message

verwandelt
metamorhpized

hatte
had

und
and

friedlich
peacefully

grinsend
grinning

in
in

seinen
his

Armen
arms

lag
laid, lay.

Die
The

Passagierin
passenger, *female*

ohne
without

Fahrschein
ticket

zu
to

suchen
search

vorgebend
pretendingly

schlenderten
strolled

die
the

beiden
both

zum
to the

zu
to, at

diesem
that

Zeitpunkt
'timepoint', moment

einer
of a

Reise
travel

menschenleeren
empty of people

Pool
pool

denn
because

als
as (as the)

Kapitän
captain

musste
musted

der
the

Kapitän
captain

nicht
not

auf
on

Schilder
signs

achten
to take care, to respect, to read (signs)

sondern
but, instead

konnte
could, *was able to*

sich
himself

anhand
using

seines
his

Gewissens
conscience, *morally*

enscheiden
decide

wohin
where to

sie
they

laufen
walk

könnten
could, potentially

und
and

oft
often

genug
enough

entschied
decided

er
he

sich
himself

frei
freely

dafür
to, for to

nicht
not

entsprechend
accordingly, correspondingly

der
the

Beschilderung
signing, the aggregate of signs attatched to a sign supporting things)

zu
to

laufen
walk

„Nun
Now

darf
may

aber
but

auch
as well

ich
I

einmal
once

Ihnen
You, *formally, plural*

eine
a

Frage
question

stellen!",
pose!"

suggerierte
suggested, ~ to let understand, to make think; not an offer, recommendation, proposition

der
the

Kapitän
captain

leicht
easily

unterwürfig
subordinarily

die
the

Hände
hands

faltend
folding

und
and

eine
a

dezent
decent

kniende
kneeling

Position
position

einnehmend
'to take in a position'

Ich
I

schwieg
remained silent

und
and

diesmal
this time

trug
wore

ich
I

ein
a

rosa
pink

Polohemd
polo shirt

Mokkassins
mokkassin shoes

und
and

eine
a

Feinrippunterhose
fine rib underwear trouser

in
in

der
which

ich
I

auch
also, as well

mein
my

Sektglas
sparkling wine glass

abstellen
to put down, to pose

konnte
could

Eine
A

nicht
not

näher
further

zu
to

präzisieren
to describe more precise, to specify

erlaubte
allowed

minimale
minimal

Bewegung
movement (body)

signalisierte
signalized

dem
the

fragenden
(questioning person)

dass
that

nun
now

seine
his

Wissensgier
greed of knowledge, not absolutely negatively connotated

aus
out of

ihm
him

heraus
out

platzen
burst, split, explode, crack;; burst

dürfte
might (forecastly)

„Nein,
"No,

sagte
said

er
he

das
that

ist
is

völlig
completely

inakzeptabel",
inaccepteable

nahm
took

seine
his

wieder
(re-); again

zurückverwandelte
backwards metamorphized

Freundin
girlfriend

entgegen
> to take; "to take contratily«, accept; take and keep

und
and

strafte
punished

sie
her

mit
with

einem
a

bitterlich
bitterly

bösen
bad

starren
rigid

Blick
look, view, staringly

„Du
You, informal

wirst
will

dich
yourself

nun
now

vor
in front of

das
the

Fernsehgerät
television device

setzen
to sit down

und
and

betrachten
regard, observe, ~consider

was
what

die
the

Menschen
humans

tun
do

die
which

gerne
likely

Automobil
automobily

fahren!".
drive

„Autokorso",
motorcade

verabschiedete
to say good bye, engoodbyed

sich
himself

der
the

Kapitän
captain

die
the

rechte
right

der
of the

Reling
deck rail

schüttelnd
shaking (the right hand)

und
and

stieg
stepped

über
over, *through*

ein
a

Fenster
window

in
into

seine
his

neben
beside

ihm
him

sitzende
sitting

Cousine
cousin

ein,
in, into, one

die
who

plötzlich
suddenly

rülpste
burped

und
and

vor
(in front of) due to

Scham
shame, ashamedness

unter
under

Deck
deck

verschwand
disappeared

wo
where

sie
she

ihren
her

Kapitän
captain

zur
to the

Welt
world

brachte
brought (gave birth to)

der
which

sogleich
immediately

bei
at, *near, (with)*

der
the

Hafenpolizei
harbour police

Anzeige
report *(monitor, display; police report)*

gegen
against

sich
himself

und
and

seine
his

Offiziere
officers

wegen
because of

Herbeiführens
cause, induce, 'to bring on'

einer
of a

spätromantischen
late romantic

Beziehung
relationship

erstattete
> report; 'to report report'
"Anzeige erstatten", *also: "to refund"*

und
and

für
for

immer
ever

das
the

Gelände
area, terrain

verließ
leave, left

Und
And

so
so

erschien
appeared

eine
a

Kapitänsmütze
captains cap

auf
on

meinem
my

Haupt
head.

„Freut
Englads, rejoices

mich
me

Kapitän"
captain

sagte
said

der
the

irische
irish

Reiseführer
travel guide

seine
his

linke
left

auf
on

meine
my

linke
left

(Schulter)
(shoulder)

schlagend
hittingly

und
and

mir
mee

ein
a

bisschen
little bit

zu
too

nah
close

fast
almost

flüsternd
whisperingly

mitzuteilen
to inform, tell, communicate, notify

dass
that

er
he

einen
a

Ständer
stand (erection)

habe
had, subjunctive, indirect speech

„Oh",
"Oh",

erinnere
remind

ich
I

mich,
myself

„Sie
You, formal

können
can

Noten
notes (music)

darauf
on it

platzieren!"
to place

Die
The

neue
new

populäre
popular

Musik
music

ist
is

wirklich
really

aus
from

den
the

siebzigern
seventies

die
the

Beatles
beatles

haben
have

so
so, 'that'

gerne
gladly

musiziert
made music

dass
that

sie
they

ganze
complete, full, whole

Hallen
halls

anmieteten
to rent

in
in

denen
which

viele
many

die
who

nicht
not

mit
with

musizieren
make music

durften
mayed, were allowed to

dazu
to it

tanzten
danced

und
and

sangen
sang

Nur
Only

wenige
few

blieben
remained

stumm
mute

da
there

stehend
standing

oder
or

kehrten
turned, orientated

sich
themselves

selbst
against

zum
to the

Publikum
audience

hin
to

die
the

Perspektive
perspective

der
the

Spielenden
music making, playing

einnehmend
to take in (perspective)

ohne
without

aber
but, though

zu
to

musizieren
make music

Per
Using, per

Gesetz
law

war
was

verboten
forbidden

worden
was

innerhalb
inside

eines
of a

Konzertes
concert

ein
a

Konzert
concert

zu
to

geben
give *(to give a concert)*

und
and

so
so

verstummten
fell silent

alle,
all those

die
who

nicht
not

die
the

Beatles
beatles

waren
were

aber
but

auch
as well

nicht
not

die
the

Beatles
beatles

sein
to be

wollten
wanted

also
thus, so

alle
all

die
who

nicht
not

begeistert
enthusiastic

waren
were

Per
Using a

Gesetz
law

wurde
was

der
the

Anschein
apparance

erweckt
to wake up

Warnungen
warnings

seien
would be

illegal
illegal

weil
because

ein
a

Jurist
lawyer

der
who

in
in

hoher
higher

beratender
consulting

Funktion
function

Regierende
reigning people, *staff*

beriet
consulted

seinen
his

Anstand
decency

insofern
insofar

verloren
lost

hatte
had

als
as

dass
that

er
he

davor
in front of, here: about

warnte
warned

Warnungen
warnings

zuzulassen
to to authorize

Der
The

dabei
with this

sitzende
sitting

Wirtschaftsminister
economic minister

kicherte
giggeled

in
into

sich
himself

hinein
~ into

in
in

seiner
his

Jugend
youth

hatte
had

er
he

viele
many

zu
to

einem
a

Bündel
bunch

gebundene
tied, bonded, united

Zigaretten
cigarettes

geraucht
smoked

und
and

stets
usually, *constantly*

ein
a

bisschen
little bit

von
of

Vaters
fathers

Gewürzvorrat
spice-, herb-, condiment-,
seasoning-stock

dazugegeben
to add to

und
and

so
then, so, thus

dachte
thought

er
he

an
at, of

Konservengläser
canned goods, glass with
canned, preserved food

die
which

man
one

öffnen
open

kann
can

ohne
without

sie
them

zuzulassen
to let closed, to to admit

und
and

dass
that

das
this

ein
a

besonders
specially

wünschenswerter
desireable

Zustand
state, *status, condition*

sei
would be

ein
a

Konservenglas
glass with preserved food

zulassen
to let close, to admit

zu
to

können
can

es
it

sozusagen
so to say

zu
to

genehmigen
authorize

Laut
relying to, according to

rief
called

ich
I

„Ich
"I

gestatte
admit, authorize

das
the

Konservenglas
glass full of preserved food

aber
but

-dosen
- cans (of pres. f.)

sind
are

auch
as well, too

in
in (in Ordnung)

Ordnung
order

und
and

verblieb
remained

an
at

dieser
this

unwirtlichen
inhospitable

kalten
cold

Stelle
place

des
of the

Schiffes
ship

der
the

Reling
deck rail

ohne
without

auch
also, even

nur
only

einen
one

Schritt
step

zu
to

laufen
walk

Zehnte
tenth

Zäsur
turning point

Rufen
Call, *verb*, Shout

Sie
you, formal

laut
loud

„Ich
"I

genehmige
authorize, *to allow formally,
potentially with a stamp*

die
the

Produktion
production

von
of

Konservendosen
~ conserving cans

Ein
A

Phänomen
phenomenon

lang
long (during)

konnte
could

ich
I

nicht
not

mehr
any more

denken
think

und
and

so
so, thus

beobachtete
observed

ich
I

mich
myself

in
in

einem
a

Handspiegel
hand mirror

wie
how

ich
I

an
at

der
the
Reling
deck rail

stehe
stand

Viele
Many

kleine
small

Handspiegel
hand mirrors

wurden
were

in
in

der
the

kleinen
small

Boutique
boutique

mit
with

dem
the

angeschlossenen
attatched

Bistro
bistro

angeboten
offered

wobei
while, whereat

in
in

dem
the

Klappdeckel
folding cap, *hinged lid*

kleine
small
Snacks
snacks

verstaut
stuffed, stored

sind
are

die
which

es
it

erlauben
allow

sich
oneself

mithilfe
using, eith the help of

dessen
these

beim
during

Essen
the Eat, meal, diner

zu
to

beobachten
observe

In
In

vielen
many

Schulen
schools

musste
musted

diese
this

Praktik
method, practice

besprochen	wenige	Nattel
to speak about	few	mobile phone (swiss talk;; national automobile telephone, abbreviation)
werden	**ein**	
to be, become	a	**nigerianischer**
		nigerian
weil	**wenig**	
because	little	**Produktion**
		production
in	**im**	
in	in the	**und**
		and
den	**Winde**	
the	wind	**verschwand**
		disappeared
Pausen	**schwankten**	
pauses	vary, sway, wave, oscillate	**sofort**
		immediately
auf	**Deshalb**	
on	Due to this, therefore	**in**
		in
den	**tauchte**	
the	dived { (appeared)	**einem**
		a
Pausenhöfen	**ein**	
playground	a	**leisen**
		small
der	**Tamagochi**	
of the	tamagochi	**Knall**
		bang
Republik	**in**	
republik	in	**der**
		which
Schülerinnen	**meiner**	
students, *female*	my	**die**
		the
und	**linken**	
and	left	**Republik**
		republic
Schüler	**Hand**	
students, *male*	hand	**Österreich**
		austria
in	**auf**	
in	up, on (appear) }	**erschuf**
		created
Handspiegel	**verwandelte**	
hand mirrors	metamorphized	**der**
		the
starrend	**sich**	
staring	itself	**Urknall**
		big bang, original bang
umherstanden	**in**	
to stand around	in	**war**
		was
und	**ein**	
and	a	**abgeschafft**
		abolished
nur	**schweizerisches**	
only	swiss	

aber
but

?
indicating a question

was
what

hat
has

der
the

Franzose
french man

in
in

der
the

Bibliothek
library

damit
with this

zu
to

tun?
do ?

Mühsam
laboriously

wendete
turned

ich
I

mich
myself

der
to the

Physiologie
physiology

der
of the

menschlichen
human

Niere
kidney

zu,
to, towards, to turn to

die
which

mir
me, to me

während
during

der
the

Schulzeit
school time

nie
never

erläutert
explicated

worden
was

war
was

Ich
I

stellte
posed

fest
hard, to constate, feststellen

dass
that

eine
one of, a

der
the

beiden
both

Venen
veins

die
which

die
the

beiden
two

Nieren
kidneys

des
of the

Menschen
human

mit
with

zu filterndem
, which has to be filtered

Blut
blood

versorgen
supplied

vom
of the

Bundesfinanzminister
federal financial minister

kontrolliert
controlled

wurde
was

und
and

per
per

Dekret
decree

vom
from the, of the

Rest
rest

des
of the

Blutkreislaufs
blood circulation

abgestellt
turned off

werden
become

konnte
could

beispielsweise
for example

wenn
when, if

die
the

Effizienz
efficiency

der
of the

Opposition
opposition

zum
to the

subordinären
subordinary

Herrschaftsmilieu
reigning milieu

oberhalb
above

der
the

Bundespressebrücke
federal press bridge

zu
too

gering
low

erschien
appeared

und
and

es
it

opportun
opportune

war
was

sich
oneself

dem
(to) the

Willen
will

der
of the

wenigen
few

nicht
not

zu
to

beugen
bow

Abgesehen
Excepting (to look away from)

davon
of this

waren
were

Arterien
arteries

kaum
barely

vorhanden
available

weil
because

die
the

Nieren
kidneys

nicht
not

wie
like

das
the

Herz
heart

über
above (over, through, per) [zu verfügen ~ to be equipped with]

Kammern
chambers

verfügten,
(to be equipped with in a material sense)

die
which

über
over, through, per

einen
a

Vorhof
forecourt, vestibulum

mit
with

Blut
blood

versorgt
supplied

würden
would be

sondern
but

nur
only

das
the

niederländische
dutch

Staatsfernsehen
states television
so
in this manner

aufgebaut
constructed

ist
is

erste
first

Kammer
chamber

zweite
second

Kammer
chamber

Sinusknoten
sinus node

Che-Guevara-Schenkel,
che-guevara-shank (~purkinje
fiber; tawara-schenkel, bundle
branches) *[wordplay]*

schließlich
finally, closingly

eine
a, one

oder
or

zwei
two

oder
or

drei
three

versorgende
supplying

Handelsrouten
trade routes

wie
how

Rotterdam
rotterdam

Rhein
rhine

und
and

Rhenania
rhenania

München
munich

Elfte
eleventh

Zäsur
turning point

Ich
I

fördere
support, *encourage, ~~stimulate~~*

die
the

Umbenennung
renaming

Berlins
of berlin

in
to

»Berlejen«.
»»Berlejen.««

Nie
Never

waren
were

die
the

Voraussetzungen
conditions, but there's a
second german word for
conditions; *settings*

so
that

schlecht
bad

um
for

an
at

der
the

Reling
deck rail

zu
to

stehen
stand

aber
but

nie
never

waren
were

sie
they

besser
better

nicht
not

nicht
not

an
at

der
the

Reling
deck rail

zu
to

stehen
stand

unter
under

Deck
deck

wurden
were

Sektgläser
sparkling wine glasses

mit
with

Kabeln
cables

verbunden
connected

auf
on

dem
the

Ausleger
boon, 'outrigger'

der
of the

Radaranlage
radar unit

besagte
said, ~besaid

zum
to a

Bündel
bundle

geschnürte
tied

Kräuterdesserts
herbal desserts

verzehrt
consumed

und
and

auf
on

der
the

Brücke
bridge

war
was

ein
a

Fitnesstudio
fitness studio

eingerichtet
arranged, installed, furnished

worden
was, 2nd degree past

in
in

dem
which

80er
80's

Jahre-Philosophie
's (decade) philosophy

mit
with

Energy-Drinks
energy drinks

und
and

diesem
that (special)

Pathos
pathos

aus
known from

den
the

Ocean's-Filmen
ocean's movies

vermengt
blended, mixed, immingled

einen
a

Duft
odoeur, odor, fragrance

aus
made of

Schweiß
sweat

Seife
sopa

und
and

Teppichbodenreiniger
carpet cleaning agent, carpet
cleaner

ergaben
result, produce

Endlich
Finally

war
was

mein
my

Spiegelbild
mirror-image, the image in the
mirror, the other reality, that
does not exist

wieder
again

da
there

auf
on

der
the

anderen
other

Seite
side

der
of the

Reling
deck rail

stand
stood

eine
a

3D-Projektion
3-D-projection

meiner
of my

selbst
self

die
which

ich
I

durch
through, using

meine
my

Bewegung
movements (physically, own
body)

steuern
steer, regulate, pilot

konnte
could

Zunächst
First, but not "Zuerst", which
would be really first, but rather
having, within an uncertain
future, the highest priority

versucht
tried

die
the

Hand
hand

zu
to

reichen
reach

wurde
was

schnell
schwiftly, quickly

deutlich
clear, obvious

dass
that

wegen
because

der
of the

Achsensymmetrie
axial symmetry

eine
a

Verbeugung
to make a bow but as a noun

deutlich
clear, obvious

mehr
more

Souveranität
sovereignity

vermitteln
~ to show, to find and state
some middle, center

würde
would

„Tolles
"Great

Produkt
product

verkaufen
sell, 'do you sell'

Sie
you, formal

stündlich?",
every hour?"

wollte
wanted

eine
a

als
as

Queen
queen

Elizabeth
Elizabeth

verkleidete
dressed up

Rentnerin
retiree, female

wissen
know

die
which

mit
with

einem
a

Monokel
monocle

und
and

ihrem
her

Ehemann
husband

eingehakt
hooked, linked in arms

natürlich,
naturally, of course

in
in

Richtung
direction

des
of the

irischen
irish

Reiseleiters
travel guide

lief
went

Sie
They

kollidierten
collided

„Pardon,
"Excuse me

gnädige
gracious, merciful, mild

Frau
Woman

auf
on

hoher
hihg

See
sea

warnt
warns

das
the

kreuzende
crossing, orthogonally arriving
ship

Schiffl",
ship!"

flüsterte
whispered

der
he, that one

während
, while, *during*

er
he

sich
himself

einige
some

Zentner
centners

Luft
air

in
in

einer
a

Brausetablette
effervescent tablet, fizzy
tablet

auflöste
resolved

und
and

sogleich
instantly, immediately,
outright

vor
in front of

den
the

Augen
eyes

des
of the

Paares
couple

verspeiste
dined, ate, ~formally

„Ich
"I

muss
must

nur
only

noch
still

eben
even

ein
a

Kabel
cable

holen
get

dann
then

können
can

wir
we

uns
us

weiter
further

unterhalten",
entertain",

schrie
screamed

er
he

dann
then

gegen
against

plötzlich
sudden

aufkommenden
upcoming, emerging

Starkwind
strong wind

Die
The

Köpfe
heads

leicht
slightly

eingezogen
contracted, to move in

liefen
went

beide
both

von
from, off

dannen
~~~thennen;; away

„Auf
On

Wiedersehen"
Resee, (good bye)

ließ
let

ich
I

mein
my

Spiegelbild
image in the mirror, but also

metaphorically

sagen
say

wegen
because

der
the

fehlenden
missing

Soundkarte
sound card

allerdings
though

musste
musted

ich
I

einen
a

Lippenleser
lip reader

bestellen
order, to demand transaction

den
which

ich
I

in
in

Form
shape

der
of the

Markendominanz
brand dominance

„Labellakarampatuuthi"
[name]

sofort
immediately
~~~

auftrug
to put on, *to carry upon*

trockene
dry

Lippen
lips

stören
disturb

eben
even

beim
when, during, in

Musizieren
making music

aber
but

das
that

wussten
knew

wiederum
again

nur
only

Blasmusiker,
musicians who blow in their instruments like saxophones, trumpets, trombones, clarinettes, oboes, flute and others

was
which

mir
to me

egal
indifferent, equal, (if not caring)

wurde
became

Die
The

Retoure
return, return shipment

wurde
was

akzeptiert
accepted

und
and

durch
through, by

einen
a

Gutschein
voucher

ersetzt
replaced

auf
on

dem
which

stand
stood

„Auf
"On

Wiedersehen!".
Resee!" (good bye)

Die
The

fremde
strange

Frau
Woman

die
which

mir
me, to me

anfangs
beginningly

das
the

Sektglas
sparkling wine glass

weggenommen
to take away

hatte
had

legte
laid

einen
a

zweiten
second

solchen
such

Gutschein
voucher

dazu
to it

und
and

ließ
let'

von
from

einem
a

Mann
man

ihre
her

Brüste
breasts

vergrößern
to make bigger

während
while

sie
she

Zirtaki
Zirtaki, a greek dance

tanzend
dancingly

einen
a

Ouzo
ouzo

nach
after

dem
the

anderen
other (ouzo), one by one, but without a certain end

die
the

Kehle
throat

hinunterkippte
to tilt downwards

„Ganz
"Completely

schön
beautiful

frech
audacious, bold, cheeky, insolent

dass
that

sie
you, formal (actually "Sie")

nicht
not

sagten
said

was
what

passieren
happen

würde
would

raunte
murmured

mein
my

Spiegelbild
mirror picture

diesmal
this time

in
in

erträglicher
tolerable

Lautstärke
loudness, volume

die
which

auf
on

dem
the

gesamten
whole

Schiff
ship

zu
to

hören
hear (~ audible, loud enough to be heard)

gewesen
was was

sein
to be

muss
must

„verwechseln
"confuse

Sie
you, *formal*

niemals
never

mehr
again

die
the

Zeitformen
tenses, tempi

'Perfekt',
perfect

'Imperfekt'
imperfect

und
and

'Plusquamperfekt'"
past perfect, pluperfect

Der
The

Arzt
doctor

antwortete
answered

dass
that

er
he

ebenfalls
also, too, likewise

keine
no

Partizipationsmöglichkeit
possibility to participate

habe
would have

weshalb
why

er
he

einen
a

Seite | page 49

Papagei
parrot

auf
on

seine
his

Schulter
shoulder

setzte
to seat

den
which

er
he

aber
but

wegen
because of

illegaler
illegal

Preisabsprachen
price agreements

in
in

sein
his

Heimatland
home country

Syrien
syria

abschieben
to push off, to deport

musste
had to

von
from

wo
where

aus
>>from

er
he

im
in the

deutschen
german

Generalkonsulat
consulate general

das
which

von
from

syrischen
syrian

Einrichtungen
[institutions], facilities

umringt
surrounded

ist
is

erneut
again, ~newly

Asyl
asylum

beantragen
request, apply for

könnte
could, dubjonctive

das
which

ihn
him

berechtigte
authorized, subj.

Frontex
frontex

maschinell
using machines

zu
to

passieren
pass

wobei
whereat

die
the

Familie
family

mithilfe
with the help of, using

von
of

Draisinen
hand cars (rails)

Bussen
busses

und
and

Fahrrädern
bikes

zurückkehren
return

musste
have to

um
in order to

Verzögerungen
delays, retardations

durch
due to

Bahnstreiks
bus strikes

zu
to

vermeiden
avoid

„Kapitän
"captain

Ahoi"
ahoi"

murmelte	**die**	**brachten**
mumbled	which	brought
mein	**sich**	**„Schießt**
my	themselves	"shoot
Bart	**sich**	**nicht**
beard	themselves	not
den	**in**	**gerade",**
which	in	straight",
ich	**wehender**	**lehnte**
I	whiffing, waving	refused (ablehnen)
sofort	**Luft**	**ich**
immediately	air	I
rasierte	**verteilend**	**ab**
shaved	to spread, spreadingly	(refuse)
„Sie	**in**	**woraufhin**
"You, formal	in	whereupon
haben	**eine**	**mir**
have	a	mee
hier	**Taube**	**die**
here	dove	the
nichts	**verwandelten**	**Taube**
nothing	metamorphized	dove
zu	**und**	**eines**
to	and	of a
suchen",	**mir**	**in**
look fot	to me	in
ergänzte	**als**	**Pink**
completed	as	pink
ich	**solche**	**vor**
I	such	in front of
an	**einen**	**die**
at	a	the
die	**Olivenzweig**	**Füße**
the	olive branch	feet
Stoppeln	**und**	**legte**
stubbles	and	to put, lay down
adressiert	**ein**	**und**
adressing to, talking to, refering to	a	and
	G36-Maschinengewehr	**eines**
	G36-machine gun	another one

in
in

transparent
transparend

auf
on

meinen
my

Rücken
back

schnallte
strapped, fixed, using a belt or cord and a clasp

„Abrüsten!",
Disarm, (demobilize)

schrie
screamed

der
the

Kapitän
captain

entrüstet
indignantly, outraged (disarmedly)

woraufhin
whereupon

ich
I

die
the

beiden
both

Läufe
drives (gun pipe things)

ineinander
into one another

verschachtelte.
interlaced

„Bittesehr
"Pleacemuch (welcome!)

eine
a

Faltung
convolution *(math.)*

nach
according to

LaPlace
[name]

und
and

DeGruyter",
[name]

stammelte
babbled, stammered

ich
I

dazu
to it

und
and

streichelte
stroked, petted

sanft
mildly

den
the

Lauf
drive, a guns pipe, actually ("walk", noun)

eines
of a

Leopard
[name]

II-Panzers
[name]-tank

der
which

sich
himself

über
over

meiner
my

rechten
right

Schulter
shoulder

positioniert
positionned

hatte
had

„Ah,
"Ah,

die
the

neue
new

Panzerfaust",
anti tank gun"

bemerkte
remarked

der
the

Kapitän
captain

im
in the (whilst)

Gehen
to walk away, also 'to walk', here: to walk away (im Gehen)

der
who

das
the

Fahrgestell
chassis

des
of the

Panzers
tank

der
which

sich
himself

hinter
behind

mir
me

versteckt
hid, hidden

hatte
had

übersah
oversaw

weil
because

auch
also, too

dieses
this, that

nun
now

nach
according to

LaPlace
[name]

und
and

DeGruyter
[name]

faltbar
convoluteable

war
was

„Danke",
Thank you

raunte
murmured

ich
I

und
and

richtete
aligned

das
the

Rohr
pipe, ~gun pipe

neu
new

aus
>>align, 'ausrichten'

indem
as, by, through

ich
I

es
it

nach
direction

unten
downwards

zog
to tear, tore* *(Goals)

woraufhin
whereupon

sich
itself

der
the

Panzer
tank

auf
on

meiner
my

Schulter
shoulder

aufliegend
rest, lying upon, ..

in
in

die
the

Höhe
height

streckte
streched

Die
The

Ketten
chains

rasselten
jangled, rattled

zufrieden
peacefully

aber
but

Öl
oil

tropfte
dropped

auf
on

mein
my

Gesicht
face

als
when

ich
I

nach
direction

oben
upwards, top, above, overhead

sah
looked

Ein
A

Grenadier
grenadier

der
who

mit
with

seinem
his

Stoffhelm
helmet made of tissue

aus
out of

der
the

Luge
hatch (properly "Luke")

lukte
~to watch out

gelobte
pledged, promised, vowed

zügig
speedily, uniterrupted, at pace

Besserung
improvement, betterment

und
and

fuhr
drove

den
the

Panzer
tank

über
above

meine
my

rechte
right

Körperhälfte
body half (alive)

das
the

rechte
right

Bein
leg

hinab
downwards

gab
gave

auf
on

Höhe
heigt

des
of the

Knies
knee

einige
some

Salutschüsse
salute shots

ab
> abgeben, to give away

und
and

verschwand
disappeared

zwischen
between

zwei
two

Dielen
boards

die
which

das
the

Deck
deck

verkleideten
encased (dressed up), hulled

„Panzer
"Tank

Ahoi",
ahoi",

murmelte
murmured

ich
I

Zwölfte
twelveth

Zäsur
turning point

Die
the

Kombüse
caboose, galley

ist
is

abseits
offsite

der
the

Reling
deck rail

Ich
I

goss
poured

mir
myself

mithilfe
with the help of

der
the

humiden
humid

Luft
air

an
at

Deck
deck

einen
a

Tee
tea

auf
>aufgießen, to infuse

den
which

ich
I

mir
myself

von
from

einem
a

Maschinisten
engineer, machinist

der
which

sich
himself

als
as

Zollinspekteur
customs inspector

verkleidet
dressed up

hatte
had

der
the

Maschinenraum
machine room, engine room

war
was

in
in

den
the

neunziger
nineties

Jahren
years

als
as

GmbH
[legal form of organization]

umfiermiert
rebranded

ausgegliedert
outsourced, divested

und
and

verkauft
sold

also
thus

privatisiert
privatized

worden
were, was

servieren
to serve

ließ
let

nicht
not

aber
but
ohne
without

darauf
thereon

aufmerksam
attentional

zu
to

machen
make

dass
that

ein
a

Betriebsrat
worker's council

gegründet
to found

werden
to be, become

darf
may

und
and

dass
that

für
for

Angestellte
emloyees

das
the

Streikrecht
right to strike

gilt,
applies

wohingegen
whereas

BeamtInnen
officials
wie
like

dieser
the

Ich-Erzähler
first person narrator

einer
one, a

ist
is

nicht
not

streiken
strike

dürfen
may

Dreizehnte
thirteenth

Zäsur
turning point, Zaesoor

Wasser
water

ist
is

ein
a

vorzügliches,
exquisite, excellent, prime

aber
but

nicht
not

immer
always

hinreichendes
sufficient

Getränk
drink

„Dieses
This

wäre
would be

alles",
everything

sagte
said

ich
I

zu
to

der
the

fremden
strange

Frau
Woman

die
which

sich
herself

sogleich
readily, directly

in
in

einen
a

Artisten
artist

verwandelte
metamorphized

der
which

mit
with

Smartphones
smartphones

jonglierend
juggling

auf
on

seinen
his

Kindern
kids

herumtrampelte
trampled around

nur
only

selten
rarely

war
was

mir
me

ein
a

Artist
artist

in
in

Camouflage
camouflage

begegnet
to meet, come across, face, encounter

ich
I

zückte
pulled out

einen
a

Notizblock
note pad

und
and

notierte
noted, wrote

die
the

Fahrgestellnummer
chassis number

des
of the

Rechengerätes
calculating device

das
which

Sie
you, *formal*

heute
today

schon
already

benutzt
used

haben
have.

„Das
"This

war
was

zwar
~indeed

so
like that

aber
but

ist
is

nicht
not

so
like that

geblieben",
remained, stayed

erzählte
told

der
the

Überwacher
surveillor

vom
of the

Ministerium
ministry

für
for

liegenbleibende
broken down (stayed lying)

Schiffe
ship

als
when

er
he

gerade
straightly

Zigarettenpause
cigarette pause

machte
made

und
and

dafür
therefor

aus
out of

seinem
his

Überwachungsbeiboot
surveillance life boat,
surveillance dinghy

ausstieg
alighted, deboarded

und
and

an
at, on

Deck
deck

kletterte
climbed

Die
The

Überwachung
surveillance

findet
takes place (finds)

von
from

einem
a

Rettungsboot
lifeboat

aus
out of; >from (out)

statt
place

Ich
I

nicke
agree in shaking the head
accordingly to the local
consensus, to nod, nodding

genauso
exactly as

wie
like

mein
my

Spiegelbild
mirror image

auf
on

der
the

anderen
other

Seite
side

der
of the

Reling
deck rail

„Der
"The

Telefonbuchverlag
phone book publishing
company

den
which

ich
I

vor
before

Ihnen
You, formal

überwachen
to surveil

musste
had to, musted

hat
had

stets
usually, steadily

eine
a, an

Auskunft
Information, disclosure

verlangt
requested

wenn
when

man one	**im** in the	**Seestraßenverkehrsordnung,** sea route traffic edict
unter under	**Ü-Wagen** surveillance-van	**nach** according to which
falschem wrong	**vor** in front of	**dem** the
Namen name	**der** the	**das** the
anrief called	**Druckerei** printing site	**Mitführen** entrainment, carrying
also thus, so	**steht!".** stands!	**von** of
wo where	**Verständnisvoll** sympathetically	**Überwachungsgeräten** surveillance equipment
Sie they	**setze** placed (to start: ansetzen, ~schedule)	**nur** only
mich me	**ich** I	**zur** in order to
zurückrufen to call back	**an** >ansetzen, to start	**Verhinderung** acoidance
könnten could, *subj.*	**zu** to	**von** of
da there	**improvisieren** improvise	**Kollisionen** collisions
kann can	**murmele** murmure	**gestattet** allowed, authorized
man one	**aber** but	**ist** is
ja yes	**versehentlich** accidentially	**„Mag** "may
kaum barely, poorly, hardly	**von** of the	**sein** be
sagen say	**Artikel** article	**aber** but
dass that	**eins** one	**die** the
man one	**der** of the	**Vorgesetzten** boss (placed in front of oneself)

interessiert
interests

das
that

nicht
not

Wir
We

müssen
must

weiter
further

überwachen
surveil

alles
all, everything

aufzeichnen
record, memorize

was
what

Sie
you, *formal*

sagen
say,

weil
because

das
that

könnte
could

ja
yes

sein
be

dass
that

die
they

vom
of the

Amt
office

einen
one

Fehler
mistake

gemacht
have made

haben
have

den
which

Sie
you, *formal*

benutzen
use

um
in order to

dem
the, to the

Amt
office

zu
to

schaden
damage, to cause a damage,
willingly cause a damage,
planingly cause a damage

Da
There, in this context

reicht
enoughs, signaling the
definition of a sufficiency

der
the

kleine
small

Verdacht
suspicion

und
and

Sie
you, *formal*

sind
are

in
in

der
the

Abwärtsspirale."
downwards spiral, downwards
guiding vicious cycle

Ich
I

puste
blow

eine
a

Möwenfeder
seagulls feather

von
off

meiner
my

Schulter
shoulder

und
and

antworte
answer

dezent
decently, restrained,
inconspicuously

empört
outraged, 'enaboved'

„Ich
I

bin
am

bereits
already

geteert
tarred

Sie
You, *formal*

können
can

mich
me

jederzeit
whenever, every time

federn!"
feather, verb

„Gut,
Good,

dann
then

mache
make

ich
I

mich
myself

'mal
once

wieder
again

auf
on

den
the

Weg
way

zurück
back

hat
has

gut
good

getan
done (a comfort is doing good)

mal
once, veiling uncertainty

mit
with

jemandem
someone

zu
to

sprechen
speak

der
who

beide
both

Perspektiven
perspectives

von
of

diesem
this

Überwachungskram
surveillance stuff

kennt
knows

aber
but

wie
how

soll
shall

ich
I

sagen
say

am
at the

Ende
end

vom
of the

Tag
day

muss
must

ich
I

meine
my

Zigaretten
cigarettes

ja
yes, *veiling untertanty here*

ooch
also, *berlin accent of 'auch'*

irjendwoher
from somewhere
(irgendwoher)

zahlen
pay

ditte
this *(das, dieses)*

schenkt
giveth, gives, donates,
presents

mir
me

keener
noone *(keiner)*

zurück
back

keene
no *(keine)*

Erstattung
refunding

von
of

Konsumgüter
consumeable goods

war
was

ooch
also, too (*auch*)

schon
already

an
at

steuerbord
starboard

sol"
like that!

ich
I

lächele
smile

dezent
decently

und
and

nicke
nod

Der
The

Überwacher
surveilor

aus
from

dem
the

Beiboot
lifeboat, dinghy

steigt
to climb

zurück
back

in
into

seinen
his

Arbeitsplatz
working place.

Sofort
Immediately

fühle
feel

ich
I

mich
myself

überwacht
surveilled

kann
can

aber
but

die
the

Situation
situation

nur
only

bedingt
conditionnedly, in limited extent

ändern
change, variate (aktively)

„Das
That

ist
is

ja
yes

als
as

hättest
would have

du
you

ooch
also (*auch*)

nich
not (*nicht*)

gleich
equally, directly (*time*)

wieder
again

weitererzählt
told further

wie
how

Muttern
mother (*muttern, sauerland accent*)

früher
earlier, in the past, before

und
and

die
the

ganzen
whole

Omasl",
grandmas

sagte
said

mein
my

Spiegelbild
mirror image

das
which

die
the

Gestalt
shape, figure

des
of the

Überwachers
surveillor

angenommen
to take to ones own sphere of
influence

hatte
had

„Holladiewaldfee"
exclamation of surprise (hello
the wood fairy)

schrie
screamed

ich
I

entsetzt
appalled, shocked

und
and

bemerkte
remarked

wie
how

die
the

Luke
hatch

des
of the

Rettungsbootes
life boat

in
in

dem
which

der
the

echte
real

Überwacher
surveillor

sich
himself

niederlassen
to let oneself down, to sit
down

wollte
wanted

wieder
again

geöffnet
opened

wurde
was

Der
the

Überwacher
surveillor

schaute
watched

heraus
out of ..

sich
himself

um
around (to watch around,
check)

ich
I

schnell
quickly

weg
away

als
as soon as

ich
I

"my
"mein

bonnie
schätzle

lies
liegt

over
oberhalb

the
vom

ocean"
ozean

pfiff
whistled

klappte
flapped

er
he

die
the

Klappe
hatch

verwirrt
confusedly

zu
closed

„Gar
even

nicht
not

so
so

leicht
easy

heutzutage
nowadays

einen
a

krisensicheren
crisis secured

Arbeitsplatz
working place

zu
to

findenl",
find

raunte
murmured

mein
my

Spiegelbild
mirror image

und
and

lehnte
lent

sich
itself

lasziv
lascivious

auf
on

die
the

Reling
deck rail

Dass
That

mein
my

Standort
location

relativ
relatively

ungünstig
unfavorable

dafür
therefor

war
was

mich
mee

einem
to a

Detail
detail

zuzuwenden
to turn towards

das
which

ich
I

nicht
not

beschreiben
decribe

kann
can

war
was

nur
only

mir
to me

bewusst
conscious, aware.

ich
I

schreibe
write

gerne
gladly

darüber
about it

dass
that

nur
only

andere
others

notieren
note, to take a note

können
can

was
which

man
one

über
about

mich
me

wissen
know

kann
can

wenn
if

keine
no

Spiegel
mirror

und
and

keine
no

Kamera-Bildgebungssysteme
camera-picture-giving-
systems

existieren
exist

Wenn
When

Sie
you, *formal*

vor
before

dem
the

Fernsehgerät
television device

stillschweigend
remaining still and silent

sitzen
sit,

arbeiten
work

Sie
you, *formal*

ein
a

bisschen
bit

wie
like

ein
a

streikender
striking

Regisseur
director (movies)

Blumen
flowers

auf
on

einer
a

Wiese
lawn

sind
are

dann
then

qualitativ
qualitatively

äquivalent
equivalent

zum
to the

wahrgenommenen
percepted

Bilde
image

aber
but

Blumen
flowers

leben
live

nicht
not

von
off

Ihrer
their, *formal*

Aufmerksamkeit
attention

sondern
but

von
from

Licht
light

Luft
air

Erde
earth

Wasser
water

an
at

Deck
deck

finde
find

ich
I

spontan
spontaneously

drei
three

davon
of them

Nein
No

zwei
two

es
it

hat
has

noch
not

nie
never

geregnet
rained

Apropos
apropos

auch
also

auf
on

dem
the

Mond
moon

hat
has

„es"
"it"

noch
still, yet

nie
never

geregnet
rained

nie
never

war was	**Nässe** wetness, humidity	**all** all
die the	**aufquoll** swell	**meine** my
Atmosphäre atmosphere	**oder** or	**Aufmerksamkeit** attention
des of the	**ein** a	**an** to
Mondes moon	**Regenbogen** rainbow	**den** the
die which	**entstanden** evolved	**zurückkehrenden** returning
nicht not	**wäre** would have	**irischen** irish
oder or	**Insofern** Insofar	**Reiseführer** travel guide
nur only	**setzte** sat	**Der** He, this one
in in	**ich** I	**hatte** had
minimalem minimal	**mich** myself	**sich** himself
Ausmaß extent	**kurz** shortly	**inzwischen** meanwhile
existiert exists	**auf** on	**eine** a
mit with	**den** the	**griechische** greec
Wasser water	**unter** under	**Flagge** flag
übersättigt over saturated	**mir** myself	**besorgt** ontained, supplied, provided, got
sodass such that	**auftauchenden** appearing	**und** and
der the	**Mond** moon	**lief** went
Boden ground	**und** and	**in** in
vor of	**verschenkte** gave away	

Adiletten
slides, shoes for bathing

zähneputzend
teeth brushingly

und
and

grüßend
greetingly

an
at

mir
me

vorbei
past (an jemandem
vorbeigehen, to pass someone
walkingly)

eine
a

Schwimmhaube
swimming cap

zierte
decorated

das
the

Haupt
head, main

und
and

eine
a

Brille
glasses, spectacles, but the
complete thing, noun

erschien
appeared

auf
on

seiner
his

Nase
nose

die
which

er
he

wie
how

eine
a

Fliege
fly

schnell
swiftly

zu
to

verscheuchen
displace, shoo, scare away,
chase

versuchte
tried

Die
The

Kreuzung
intersection

zweier
of two

Handelswege
trade routes

also
thus

nicht
not

etwa
some

ein
a

Zwiesel
[object]

sondern
but

eine
a

alte
old

Stadt
town

Rom
rome

Die
The

symbolische
symbolic

Bedeutung
meaning

der
of the

Stadt
town

auf
on

den
the

Hügeln
hills

die
which

Namen
names

tragen
have, carry

war
was

noch
not

nie
never

so
that

Seite | page 59

ungebrochen
unbroken

wie
how

gestern
yesterday

noch
still

Das
the

Impfzentrum
vaccination central

am
at the

Vatikan
vatican

war
was

noch
still

immer
always, (remainingly)

geöffnet
opened

aus
due to

Furcht
fear

vor
of

anlandenden
landing, disembarking

Verschwörungstheoretikern,
cinspiracy theorists

Heiligen
holy

und
and

um
in order to

anlegende
landing

befreundete
being friends and friendly

wie
how

verfeindete
antagonized

Kirchenschiffe
naves (church ships)

versorgen
supply, provide, accomodate,
to take care of

zu
to

können
can, be able to

Ich
I

rechnete
calculated

damit
with it

nächstes
next

Silvester
silvester

an
at the

dieser
this

Reling
deck rail

zu
to

verbringen
spend, spend time

und
and

kalkulierte
calculated

grob
roughly

wie
how

viele
many

Sektgläser
sparkling wine glasses

die
the

Küche
kitchen

mit
with

IP-Adressen
IP-adresses

verknüpfen
to connect

wird
will

müssen
have to

bevor
before

das
the

Protokoll
protocol

erneut
again

geändert
channged

werden
to be

muss
has to

Die
The

bleiern
leadenly

schweren
heavy

Beine
legs

ich
I

hatte
had

mir
myself

untersagt
forbid

zu
to

sitzen
sit

zeugten
confessed, showed, revealed

vom
of the

Genie
genius

des
of the

Hafenmeisters
harbour master

der
who, which

das
the

Kreuzfahrtschiff
cruise ship

ein
a

wenig
little

Salzwasser
salt water

bunkern
to bunker, store

ließ
let

aber
but

auch
also

eigene
own

Reserven
reserves

anlegen
to build up

durfte
may, was allowed to

Dafür
Therefore

wurde
was

Regenwasser
rainwater

gesammelt
collected

per
per

Destillation
destillation

von
of the

Mineralien
minerals

gereinigt
cleared

zur
to the

Kühlung
chilling

des
of the

Sektgläser-Rechenzentrums
sparkling-wine-glasses-
calculation-center

verwendet
used

und
and

schließlich
finally

mit
with

Nitritpökelsalz
nitrite pickle salt

versetzt
(is being put to something)

das
which

in
in

der
the

Küche
kitchen

eingelagert
stored

wurde
was

für
for

den
the

Fall
case

dass
that

ein
a

Fisch
fish

mit with	**nie** never	**komplexe** complex
dem the	**langweilig** boring	**Reaktionen** reactions
Schiff ship	**da** as	**umzusetzen** to to implement
kollidierte collided	**alle** all	**verstand** understood, kew how to
und and	**Bewerbungen** applications (job)	**Leider** Unfortunately
eingelagert stored	**scheitern** fail	**brach** broke
werden to be, become	**würden** would	**dabei** during this
musste had to, musted	**erlaubte** allowed	**ein** a
Da As	**ich** I	**Stück** piece
ich I	**mir** myself	**der** of the
an at	**eine** a	**Bordwand** board wall
der the	**Art** kind of	**weg** away
Reling deck rail	**Resonanzmaschine** resonance machine	**die** which
selbstverständlich of course	**zu** to	**die** the
arbeitslos workless	**erschaffen** create	**Kabinen** cabins
zu to	**die** which	**von** off
bleiben remain	**meine** my	**Deck** deck
hatte had	**Aktionen** actions	**trennten** separated
wurde was, became	**in** in	**weshalb** why
mir to me	**relativ** relatively	**ich** I

plötzlich
suddenly

einen
a

Teil
part

des
of the

Proberaumes
exercising room

für
for

Musiker
musicians

einsehen
to look into

konnte
could

Damit
Such that

die
the

Instrumente
instruments

nicht
not

nassregneten
to be rained wet

zauberte
magiqued

ein
a

Arzt
doctor, physicist

der
which

sich
himself

mit
with

einem
a

Lehrer
teacher

verwechselte
confused

spontan
spontaneously

eine
a

neue
new

solche
such

Wand
wall

herbei
to here

was
which

mich
me

überraschte
surprised

aber
but

ich
I

lasse
let'

mir
myself

solches
such

wie
like

Sie
you, *formal*

nicht
not

mehr
any more

anmerken
observe (to not allow others to
understand one's reaction)

Am
At the

Anzug
suit

erkannte
recognized

man
one

dass
that

der
the

Arzt
physicist

mit
with

den
the

hohen
high

Künsten
arts

der
of the

Zauberei
magic

vertraut
familiar

war
was

denn
because

seine
his

Bewegungen
movements, body

waren
were

ruhig
silent (smooth), calm

und
and

gelassen
equanimous, silent

während
while

aber
but

ein
a

leichtes
slight

Zittern
trembling

seinen
his

Kopf
head

bewegte
moved

die
the

Frequenz
frequency

des
of the

Zitterns
trembling

betrug
amounted

etwa
around

Schwingungen
oscillations

pro
per

Minute
minute

und
and

wurde
was

durch
through

eine
a

Horde
horde

von
of

einundzwanzig
twentyone

hinter
behind

ihm
him

laufenden
walking

als
as

Zwergen
dwarfs

verkleideten
dressed up

Kindergartenkindern
kindergarten kids

begleitet
accompaigned

die
which, who

riefen
called

"Hoch
"high

die
the

Tassen
cups

fliegen
fly

lassen
let

wir
we

sind
are

die
the

Krabbelgruppe
crawl group

Afghanistan!"
afghanistan

(ZITATI)
(QUOTE!)

In
In

ihren
their, *designating a group*

kleinen
small

Körben
baskets

trugen
carried, wore

die
the

Kinder
kids

Produkte
products

bei
with

sich
themselves

die
which

interessante
interesting

Eigenschaften
attributes, characteristics

aufwiesen
to hold, exhibit, show, offer

die
which

ich
I

nun
now

für
for

die
the

chinesische
chinese

Sprache
language

optimieren
optimize

möchte
want

Ziege
goat

Milch
milk

Fermentat
fermenting object

Käse
cheese

Salz
salt

Wasser
water

Schminke
Make Up

Gesicht
face

Clown
clown

Papier
paper

Tinte
ink

Tag
day

Bericht
report

Die
The

Furcht
fear

vor
(in front) of

dem
the

Blitzeinschlag
thunder impact

Goethes
of Goethe

in
in, into

die
the

Reling
deck rail

ließ
let, *past*

mich
me

einige
some

wenige
few

Zentimeter
centimeters

nach
to, direction

rechts
right

von
of

der
the

Reling
deck rail

weg
away

beugen
bow, bend

was
which

sogleich
readily

von
of

der
the

Reisegruppe
travel group

quittiert
acknowledged

wurde
was

eine
a

wilde
wild

Reporterin
reporter, *female*

hatte
had

dem
to the

anderen
other

Reiseleiter
travel guide

das
the

Anführungszeichenschild
quotation mark sign

entrissen
snatched, ripped away

und
and

führte
guided

die
the

Gruppen
groups

an
to

mich
me

heran
to me

"Und
And

hier
here

sehen
see

Sie
you, *formal*

denjenigen
the one

der
who

sich
himself

vor
regarding

Blitzen
thunders

fürchtet
fears

weshalb
why, *reason*

Sie
you, *formal*

ihm
him

gerne
likely

Angst
fear

machen
make

dürfen
may

und
and

alles
everything

andere
else

ist
is

mir
me

egal
equal

wir
we

gehen
walk

weiter".
on, further

Die
The

Reiseleiterin
travel guide

lief
went

dem
the

irischen
irish

Reiseleiter
travel guide

hinterher
behind, attachedly

verliebte
fell in love

sich
herself

in
in

ihn
him

und
and

bekam
received (gave birth to)

mit
with

seiner
his

Armbanduhr
wristwatch

ein
a

Kind
kid

das
which

sogleich
immediately

zum
to the

Gottkaiserkapitänreiseführer
god kaiser captain travel guide

erkiert
chose, elected, nominated

wurde
was

Gerne
gladly

blieb
remained

die
the

Gruppe
group

bei
near, with

mir
me

stehen
stand

und
and

verband
(closed, such that there is no optical impression)

mir
to me, me

zunächst
almoste first

die
the

Augen
eyes

mithilfe
with the help of, using

einer
a

Gesichtsmaske
face mask

und
and

Vogelkot
bird excrement

der
which

mithilfe
with the help, using

eines
of a

eigens
specifically, "ownly", especially

entwickelten
developped

Apparates
device

völlig
completely

entkeimt
sterilized

worden
was was

war
was

und
and

nur
only

dezent
decently

roch
smelled

Ein
A

herbeigeeilter
hurried to the place

Matrose
sailor

in
in

ziviler
civil

Kleidung
clothing

und
and

grauem
grey

Antlitz
visage

bot
offered

mir
to me

ein
a

Zeitungspapier
newspaper

an
anbieten - to offer

mit
with

dem
which

ich
I

den
the

vorherigen
previous

Zustand
state, conditions

wiederherstellen
restore, re-establish, rebuild, reconstruct

könne
could, subj.

ich
I

müsse
would have to

ihm
him

nur
only

meinen
my

Namen
name

nennen
name, to call, to say

Ich
I

nannte
named, said

Name
name

und
and

Adresse
adress

und
and

verprügelte
battered

die
the

anstehende
pending

Gruppe
group

mit
with

der
the

gereichten
given, handed out

Zeitung
newspaper

so
as, so

lange
long

bis
until

mir
to me

jemand
someone

die
the

Maske
mask

abnahm
took off

und
and

das
the

Gesicht
face

reinigte
cleaned

Vierzehnte
fourteenth

Zäsur
caesur

Das
The

mit
with

der
the

Schreibblockade
writing bloquade

Ich
I

las
red, read
ein
a

Buch
book

mit
with

dem
the

Anfang
Beginning

»Ein
»A

sattes
rich, full, saturated

Schwarz
black

so
just

wie
like

wenn
when

man
one

Kohlestaub
coal dust

auf
on

eine
a

geweißelte
whitened (painted)

Wand
wall

pustet
blows

zeichnete
featured

mein
my

kaffeesatzartig
coffee ground-like

Erbrochenes
vomited

aus
auszeichnen - featured

Pralinen
pralines

mit
with

Espressofüllung.
espresso filling

Ich
I

stehe
stand

an
at

der
the

Reling
deck rail

und
and

kotze
chuck up

ins
into the

blaue
blue

Wasser
water

Wegen
Because of

"my
"mein

Bonnie
Schätzchen

lies
liegt

over
oberhalb

the
des

ocean"
Ozeans

schippere
cruise

ich
I

über
over

das
the

Mittelmeer
mediterrean sea

Das
The

Mittelmeer
mediterrean sea

ist
is

übrigens
by the way

gar
at all

kein
no

Ozean
ocean

die
the

Begrüßungsrunde
salutation, greeting, get to
know each other - round

musste
had to

ohne
without

mich
me

stattgefunden
to take place

haben
have

Jedenfalls
anyway

lief
went

bevor
before

ich
I

jemanden
someone

ansprechen
to start talking to someone,
starting a conversation in
order to ask or to get to know
something

konnte
could

Niemand
noone

schlangengleich
snake-like

grazielst
most gracile possible

auf
on, direction

mich
me

zu
to

übergibt
passes

mir
me

sanft
softly

zwei
two

Sektgläser
sparkling wine glasses

wirft
throws

das
the

Tablet
tablet, tray

spielerisch
playfully

in
into

die
the

Höhe
height

und
and

schleicht
tiptoes

seekrank
seasick

in
in

Richtung
direction

Bistro.
bistro

Wegen
because of

der
the

Übelkeit
vomiting, nausea, sickness

konnte
could

man
one

uns
us

glatt
plain, in the sense of easily,
spontaneously

für
for

Geschwister
ciblings

halten
hold, (to assume: »to hold
something for..«)

mit
with

einem
a, one

Gendefekt
genetic defect

für
for

besonders
especially

blasse
pale

Haut
skin

Bruder
brother

und
and

Schwester
sister

auf
on

ewig
eternily

anders
different

Vor
In front of

uns
us

im
in the

Fahrwasser
fairway, shipping water

würde
would

irgendwann
somewhen

ein
a

anderes
different

Schiff
ship

mit
with

ebenfalls
likewise

anderen
different

Gästen
passengers, guests

und
and

einem
a

alten
old

Kapitän
captain

entgegenkommen
to meet, moving in opposite directions

für
for

einen
a

Monat
month

lang
long

passieren
pass

die
the

Wolken
clouds

aufreißen
tear open

und
and

man
one

fotografierte
fotographed

sich
oneself

in
in

blankem
blank

Entsetzen
fright, horror

von
of

der
the

Vergänglichkeit
fugacity

der
of the

Begegnung
meeting

und
and

würde
would

uns
us

irgendwann
somewhen

ein
a

Passepartout
passepartout

umlegen
tp lay around

und
and

warf
threw

es
it

als
as

„zu
too

realistisch"
realistic

über
over

Bord
board

Der
the

Überwacher
surveillor

aus
from

dem
the

Rettungsboot
life boat

fing
catched

es
it

auf
up

und
and

baute
build

damit
with it

ein
a

riesiges
huge

Papierschiff
paper ship

das
which

über
over, above

dieses
this

und
and

das
that

Nachbarschiff
neighbouring ship

passte
matched

allerdings
but, however, though, admittedly

war
was

dadurch
due to this

vollständige
complete, from completeness, thoroughly

Dunkelheit
darkness

an
on

Bord
board

ober
above

wie
like

unter
under

Deck
deck

eingetreten
entered, occured

weshalb
which is why

ein
a

Passagier
passenger

an
at

Steuerbord
starboard

das
the

Papierschiff
paper ship

in
in

Brand
Fire

setzte
sat *(down)*

In
In

jedem
every

Augenblick
blink of an eye

konnte
could

mich
me

ein
a

herabfallendes
falling down

brennendes
burning

Stück
piece

Papier
paper

erschlagen
hit dead

aber
but

ich
I

darf
may

mithilfe
using, with the help of

von
of

lauten
loud

Gebeten
prayers

einen
a

Luftstrom
air stream

erzeugen
produce, create

der
which

die
the

Aschefetzen
ash frazzles

jenseits
beyond

der
the

Reling
deck rail

verschob
moved, pushed, displaced;

Viele
Many

PassagierInnen
passengers, gendered

machten
made

das
that

so
like described

mit
with, to join in: mitmachen

ein
a

sehr
very

lauter
loud

Chor
choir

entstand
arose

wegen
because of

des
the

brennenden
burning

Papierschiffes
paper ship

Deshalb
Due to this

muss
has to

man
one

stets
usually, constantly, steadily

fotogen
photogenic, filmeable

an
at

der
the

Reling
deck rail

stehen
stand

Das
That

belastet
strains, stresses, loads, burdens

auch
also

psychisch
psychically

aber
but

wie
how

kann
can

man
one

sich
oneself

in
in

so
such

einer
a

Situation
situation

kennenlernen
to get to know each other

Offensichtlich
Obviously

ist
is

dass
that

dafür
for this

immer
always

alle
everybody

an
at

der
the

Reling
deck rail

stehen
stand

müssen
must

die
the

linke
left

Hand
hand

sofern
as far as

möglich
possible

auf
on

den
the

Handlauf
hand rail

gelegt
laid down

und
and

den
the

Blick
look

behutsam
cautious, gingerly

stur
stubborn

nach
direction

vorn'
forwards

gewandt
turned

so
in this situation, like this

kann
can

man
one

den
the

Trubel
hustle, confusion, turbulences

an
on

Deck
deck

gut
well, good

erleben
experience

real
echt

time
Zeit

surveillance
Überwachung

real
echt

time
Zeit

surveillance
Überwachung

real-time
Echtzeit

surveillance
Überwachung

abuse
Missbrauch

abuse
Missbrauch

abuse
Missbrauch

non-information
Nicht-Mitteilung

torture
Folter

president
Präsident

president
Präsident

Es
It

war
was

einmal
once

vor
before [ago]

vielen
many

vielen
many

Jahren,
years

Zäsur
Zaesur

fünfzehn
fifteen

Dies
Thees, (this)

ist
is

kein
no

Märchen
fairytale

ich
I

wiederhole
repeat

dies
this

ist
is

kein
noo

Märchen
fairytale

Meine
My

Schotten
scots

bleiben
remain

dicht
tight, closed, don't let enter light

Weil
Because

Einfältigkeit
simple-mindedness

ein
a

Verlust
loss

ist
is

Die
The

erste
first

nicht-schwarz/rot/güldene
not-black-red-gølden

Partei
Party, political, Partei

in
in

Deutschland
germany

die
the

grüne
green

Partei
Partei, party, political

hat
had

ein
a

Problem
problem

mit
with

weiteren
further

solchen
such

Parteien
parties

die
which

zügellos
dissolute

ihre
their

populistischen
populist

Vorstellungen
imaginations

in
in

politische
political

Forderungen
demands

umformulieren
reformulate, *gramatically*

ohne
without

zu
to

prüfen
check

ob
whether

die
they

überhaupt
at all, even

in
in

Einklang
unison, accord

mit
with

internationalem
international

Recht
right, laws

stehen
stand

Es
It

lohnt
worthes, it is profiteable

sich
itself

eine
a

Potenz
power *(a to the power of b)*, *also: ability, force*

von
of

zwei
two

das
that

sind
are

die
the

0-1-
0-1-

Zäsur
Zaesur

sechzehn
sixteen

Die
The

Kommunikation
communication

war
was

fast
almost

noch
still, yet

nie
never

zuvor
before

auf
on

der
the

Ebene
level

des
of the

binären
binary

Zahlensystems
number system

angelangt
reached, landed

Name
Name

schwieg
remained silent

Von
Of

ihrer
their

Warte
lookout

aus
out (lookout-out, out of the lookout out out)

hätte
would have

ich
I

nur
only

eine
one

brennende
burning

Ziege
goat

entdecken
discover

und
and

durch
throug

schwebende
hovering

Seifenblasen
soap bubbles

springen
jump

lassen
let

müssen
must

aber
but

ich
I

verneinte
negated

ich
I

würde
would

permanent
permanently

den
the

Kopf
head

schütteln
shake

müssen
have to

"dem
this, to this

musst
have to, must

du
you

dich
yourself

beugen".
bow

Von
Of

der
the

Brücke
bridge

aus
out

sieht
sees

man
one

zu
too

viel
much

ich
I

sage
say

wir
we

machen
make

eine
a

Fantasiereise
fantasy travel

und
and

ich
I

zeige
show

dir
you

die
the

schönsten
most beautiful

Erkenntnisse
Insights

der
of the

Geschichte
History

„ist
Is

für
for

unseren
our

nüchternen
sober

Schiffbruch",
wreckage

sprach
spoke

Name
Name

mit
with

nicht
not

überspieltem
overrode

Stolz
pride, *proudness*

„mit
with

Tiger"
tiger

stottere
stuttered

ich
I

leise
quietly

um
in order to

mehr
more

zu
to

erfahren
learn, find, experience

Nun
Now

flüstert
whispers

Name
Name:

sie
she

sah
looked

mir
me

in
in

die
the

glasigen
glassy, vitric

Augen
eyes

und
and

ich
I

sah
saw

mein
my

Spiegelbild
mirror-image

in
in

ihren
hers

Aus
out of, *here: caused by;
indicating a reason*

Spaß
fun

setzte
posed, sat

sie
she

den
the

profundgewichtigen
profoundly weighting
(neologism)

Tiger
tiger

gekonnt
skillfully

aber
but, though

ungeschickt
clumsy

zwischen
between

unsere
our

Füße
feet

ohne
without

mich
me

aus
out of

den
the

Augen
eyes

zu
to

lassen
let

„Also
Right, Well

wirklich
really

bitte
please

nicht
not

der
the, this one

ist
is

echt
really

gefährlich",
dangerous

sofort
immediately

ist
is

klar
clear

dass
that

ich
I

genau
exactly

die
the

richtigen
right

den
the

richtigen
right

Ton
sound, note

440
440

Hertz
hertz

getroffen
hit'

habe
have

ist
is

so
just like indicated

Im
in the

goldenen
golden

Käfig
cage

sitzt
sits

ein
a

anderer
other

weißer
white

Tiger
tiger

für
for

avantgardistische
avant-garde

Frauen
women

unter
under

50
fifty

der
the

Name
name

erwartungsvoll
expectant, full of expectations

missachtet
ignores, disesteems

den
the

Name
name

erwartungsvoll
expectant, full of expectations

ignoriert
ignores

Er
He

bedeckt
covers

den
the

Käfig
cage

mit
with

einem
a

Kuvert
envelope

das
which

er
he

aus
out

dem
the

Futter
lining

seines
of his

Mantels
coat

herausgerissen
had ripped out, teared out

Seite | page 73 - 74

hatte
had

ich
I

resigniere
resign

„gehe
walk, *here: assume*

davon
off, away

aus
out of

dass
that *(I assume, that)*

Du
you

dich
yourself

der
to the

Situation
situation

entziehen
withdraw

willst",
want

meint
means

der
the

Tiger
tiger

„woher
where from

will
wants

sie
she

das
this

wissen",
know

denke
think

ich,
I

„ich
I

werde
will

dir
you

den
the

weißen
white

Tiger
tiger

wegnehmen",
to take away

sagt
says

Name,
name,

ein
a

flotter
swift, zippy, fast

Spruch
slogan

und
and

dann,
then

„Ciao
ciao

Kakao"
cocoa

wie
how

im
in the

Regensburger
rains burghish

Abendblatt
evening journal

geht
goes

das
that

denn
then

immer
always

so
like that

weiter
further

„Was
What

war
was

denn?",
thenn?

ich
I

sitze
sit

mit
with

verschränkten
folded

Armen
arms

auf
on

ihrem
their

Koffer
suitcase

und
and

erschaudere
cringe

im
in the

Moment
moment

des
of the

Kennenlernens
to get to know each other

dieser
of this

Frau
women

hilflos
helpless

bis
until

nachher
later

gestern
yesterday

dort
there

kommen
comes

Rehlinge
deerlings / deer rails (PUN)

dauert
dureth

es
it

noch
still

ewig
eternally

sogar
even

die
the

Kuh
cow

hat
has

die
the

Brücke
bridge

verlassen
left

und
and

wartet
waits

gelangweilt
boredly

während
while

sie
she

gelangweilt
boredly

mit
with

den
the

Füßen
feet

gegen
against

den
the

Käfig
cage

tippt
tip *(to touch with fingers)*

nur
only

damit
so that

sie
she

„Jackpot
Jackpot

meines
of my

Lebens
life

nie
never

wieder
again

umzusetzen"
to earn, implement, relocate

in
in

den
the

Maschinenraum
machine room

brüllt
yell, roar *(lion)*

tragen
wear

Name
name

und
and

ich
I

plötzlich
suddenly

beide
both

Krawatten
cravats, ties

Name	name
repariert	repared
gelangweilt	boredly
ihr	her
Handy	smartphone
wirft	throws
dessen	its
Hülle	hull, cover, casing
über	over
Bord	board
und	and
angelt	angles, fishes
einen	a
Maulschlüssel	wrench
aus	out of
dem	to the, of the
Meer	sea
in	in
diesem	this
Augenblick	blink of an eye, moment
beginnt	begins
die	the
Reise	journey
erst	firstly
richtig	corretly
»das	the
Leben	life
lässt	lets
sich	itself
nicht	not
mehr	any more
in	in
ein	a
davor	before
in	in
ein	a
„davor"	before
erinnern	remind
einordnen	classify
und	and
ein	a
„danach",	after
danach	later, using this attribution
lässt	lets
es	it
sich	itself
nicht	not
mehr	any more
unterscheiden.«,	differenciate, distinguish
stammelte	spluttered, stammered, babbled
ein	a
Matrose	sailor
Das	That
fühlt	feels
sich	itself
gleich	equally
an	on
aber	but
ist	is

nicht
not

mehr
any more

dasselbe
thesame, the same

damit
with this

hatte
had

ich
I

nicht
not

gerechnet
calculated

am
at the

Anfang
beginning

an
at

genau
exactly

der
the

gleichen
same

Stelle
place

an
at

der
which

wir
we

uns
ourselves

vor
before

acht
eight

Tagen
days

die
the

Seele
soul

aus
out

dem
of

Leib
body, belly, a little spiritual

kotzten
threw up

stehen
stood

wir
we

an
at

der
the

Reling
deck rail

Rotterdam
rotterdam

nun
now

sagt
says

Name
name

„die
the

gleichen
same

Gäste
guests

haben
have

einfach
easily

eine
a

Woche
week

lang
long

eine
a

neue
new

Sprache
language

erfunden
invented

das
that

war
was

sicher
surely

anstrengend!".
stressful, rather "effortful",
physically and/or mentally
exhausting

Ich
I

verspanne
tense up, tensions inside the
body due to stress

als
when

ich
I

mir
myself

ausmale envisionned (to paint out)	**Name** name	**Loch** hole
was what	**meinte** meant	**ab** >>abzeichnen
seit since	**„da** there	**wie** how, like, comparingly
der the	**waren** were	**das** the one
Abfahrt departure	**so** so	**was** which
alles all	**leckere** tasty	**Homer** homer
aufgegeben abandonned	**materioschka** materioshka (russian kindof doll)	**unter** under
wurde was	**Pralinen** pralins	**die** the
was what	**drinl"** inside	**Spüle** sink
alles all	**„Mist",** ~ crap it	**seiner** of his
spurlos traceless	**sage** say	**Frau** wife
verschwand disappeared	**ich** I	**installiert** installed
meinen my	**„am** at the	**hatte** had
Koffer suitcase	**Horizont** horizon	**und** and
hatte had	**zeichnete** abzeichnen:: emerged, to show up, let' understand	**versehentlich** accidentially
man one	**sich** itself	**weite** wide, far
bereits already	**ein** a	**Teile** parts
über over	**einziges** sole, only	**des** of the
Bord board	**schwarzes** black	**Zeichentrickuniversums** comic universe
geworfen thrown		**verschlang"** swallowed up

immer
always

mehr
more

Gäste
guests

beginnen
begin

zu
to

weinen
cry

irgendwo
somewhere

implodiert
implodes

eine
a

Bildröhre
cathode ray, picture tube,
television tube

eine
a

Reihe
row

Seeminen
sea mines

detoniert
detonates

und
and

spendet
spends, ((\donates))

reichlich
plenty of

Beleuchtung
leighting

Vom
From the

Hochsitz
high seat

aus
out

pfeift
whistles

ein
a

eingeschlafener
slept in

Schiedsrichter
referee

lasziv
lascivious

die
the

Moldau
moldau

während
while

zwei
two

zivil
civilly

gekleidete
dressed

Soldaten
soldiers

mit
with

einer
a

Handgranate
hand grenade

Entschärfen
deactivate, disarm

spielten
played

Ein
A

betrunkener
drunk

Kameramann
camera man

müht
labors, struggles, endeavours

sich
himself

sichtlich
visibly

ab
off (sich abmühen, ~ to
struggle off)

die
the

Szenerie
scenery

mit
with

Knicklichtern
bending lights, these tubes

auszuleuchten
light, illuminate a room etc.

während
during

er
he

sie
her

filmt.
films

Jesus
"Jesus

guck'
look

weg
away

gleich
soon (equally)

brennt's
burns it

Im
In the

Feuer
fire

beredtes
eloquent, silver-tongued

Schweigen
silence, remaining silent

Fundort
find spot

verlassen
left, to leave

Abflug
departure

ab
from

Rotterdam
rotterdam

eine
one

Minute
minute

nach
after

Anlandung.
landing

Sie
They

bedeuten
imply, let know, (to point to), depictingly

mir
to me

subtil
subtly

ich
I

sei
would be

hier
here

nicht
not

erwünscht
desired, welcomed

Name
Name

und
and

Name
name

löschen
delete

nach
at will

Belieben
at will

Beweisfotos
pictures of proof

der
of the

Verzweiflung
despair

an
at

Bord
board

Wo
Where

Name
name

ist
is

weiß
knows

ich
I

dank
thanks to

ich
I

halte
hold

mich
myself

um
for

Hilfe
help

rufend
calling, shouting

auf
on

dem
the

Zwischendeck
intermediate deck

auf
on

da
because

oben
above

Eis
ice

genascht
nibbled

und
and

sich
oneself

unten
lower

Chilies
chilies

in
in

die
the

Augen
eyes

gerieben
rubbed

werden
are

Um
In order to

auf
on, regarding

alle
all the, every

Kosten
cost

vorbereitet
prepared

zu
to

sein
be

empfiehlt
recommends

es
it

sich
itself

Devisen
foreign exchange, currency

aller
of all

Nachbarländer
neighbour countries

vorrätig
stored

zu
to

haben
have

das
that

gehört
belongs to

zum
to the

Allgemeinwissen
general knowledge

in
in

internationalen
international

Gewässern
waters

Name
Name

tippelt
walks on toes

unruhig
agitatedly

auf
on

der
the

Stelle
place

wie
how

eine
a

geteerte
tared

Feder
feather

Wer
Who

schon
already

gepackt
packed

hat
had

macht
makes

es
it

sich
to self

gemütlich
comfortable

wer
who

noch
still

Pfandflaschen
returneable bottle

hat
has

der
the

donnert
fulminates, throws grossly

sie
them

gut
good

hörbar
audible, heareable

in
into

den
the

Automaten
automat, machine

unter
under

Deck
deck

so
such

dass
that

alle
all

das
the

Knistern
spattering, sizzling, cracking noise

des
of the

Pfandguts
returneable bottle goods

hören
hear

können
can

wenn
when

es
it

gequetscht
squeezed

wird
is being

Ankunft
arrival

Abreise
departure

am
at the

Zielhafen
destination harbour

Rotterdam
rotterdam

in
in

einer
one

Minute
minute

Koffer
suitcase

zum
to the

Verwahren
storing, keeping, coffering

einfach
easily

über
over

Bord
board

werfen
throw

Das
that

war
was

der
the

achte
eigth

Tag
day

Für
for

alle
all

anderen
others

gibt
giveth

es
it

woanders
otherwhere, somewhere else

auch
also, too, likewise

etwas
something

Tequila
tequila

in
in

Fässern
barrels

Mit
with

einer
a

leichten
slight

Feder
feather

die
which

er
he

vergessen
forgot

hat
has

war
was

er
he

zu
to

der
that

Zeit
time

Schreiber
Writer

Draußen
Outside

vor
in front of

der
the

Garage
garage

steht
stands

die
the

Butter
butter

weil
because

oben
above, up

d'rüber
above

ein
a

Bordell
bordell

war
was

sieht
looks, *sees*

man
one

überall
everywhere

kleine
small

Pailletten
pailettes

Weil
because

sie
she

Papierstücke
paper pieces

aneinander
against each other

klebt
glued

sitzt
sits

sie
she

unter
under

einer
a

Arbeitsplatte
worktop

mit
with

einem
a

frisch
fresh

gefärbten
coloured

Sockenpaar
pair of socks

und
and

einer
a

Unterhose
underwear trouser

auf
on

dem
the

Kopf
head

Der
The

Riese
giant

beackert
to work on, *(from acker, acre)*
common speech

völlig
completely

unvernünftig
irrationally

die
the

Schmuckschatulle
jewel case

des
of the

Neffen
nephew

aber
but

wie
how

gesagt
said

„Da
as

ich
I

mit
with

dir
you

nicht
not

so
so

übereinstimme
agree

hätte
would have

ich
I

die
the

konsensuale
consensual

Ableitung
deduction

fremder
of strange

Tatsachen
facts

dann
then

genau
exactly

gekannt"
known

als
as

Rentnerin
retiree, *female*

bist
are

du
you

eine
a

Quasseltasche
'jabber pocket' (talks much)

erzähle
tell

ich
I

dir
you

nicht
not

die
the

ganze
whole

Zeit
time

wie
how

es
it

ist
is

die
the

Urenkel
great grandchildren

kennenzulernen
to get to know

Siebzehnte
seventeenth

Zäsur
zaesur

Das
this

war
was

mein
my

Fehler
mistake

Die
The

deutsche
german

Printproduktnorm
print product norm

für
for

politikbezogene
related to politics

Inhalte
contents

aus
out of (from)

dem
the

Jahr
year

2024
2024

in
in

ihrer
her

ersten
first

Version
Version

1.1
1.1

erläutert
explicates

uns
us

alle
all

Ansprüche
demands, requirements

die
which

das
the

hiesige
around here, in this area

Volk
population, people

an
at, regarding, to

einen
a

vorzüglichen
extraordinary

Kanzler
chancellor

haben
have

darf
may

und
and

welche
which

es
it

haben
have

muss
must, has to

DppN
gppn

pbzi
[related to politics]

2024-1.1
2024-1.1

****
\\

EU-de
EU-de

Mindestanspruchsberechtigung:
minimal attention/demand/expectation eligibility

volljährig
of full age

Schulabschluss
school graduation

Maximalanspruchsüberschreitungsniveau
maximal claim/requirement exceedance level

Alle
All, every

Vorstrafen
conviction

auch
as well, too

kirchlich
churchly, ecclesiastical

gebüßt
purged

reicher
richer

als
than

der
the

Bundespräsident
federal president

Kunde
customer

von
of

zwei
two

oder
or

mehr
more

Banken
financial institutes

Buch
book

veröffentlicht
published

ohne
without

parteiinternen
party internal

Machtkampf
fight for (about) power

zu
to

Relevanz
relevance

gelangt
achieved

Alkoholiker
alcoholician

ehemaliger
former

Alkoholiker
alcoholician

Jurist
lawyer

weiterer
further

akademischer
academic

Abschluss
degree

Schulnoten
school marks, grades

eins
one (1; A)

in
in

Sport,
sports

Sozialkunde
social studies

und
and

Religion
religion

beliebt
beloved

unbeliebt
unbeloved

Brillenträgerin
wearer of glasses

gendert
changed

Achtzehnte
eightteenth

Zäsur
zaesur, turning point

Finden
find *(imperativ)*

Sie
you, *formal*

einen
a

Kanzlerkandidaten
chancellor candidate

auf,
'to find up', to find in a certain
place

verweisen
relegate, point towards

Sie
you, *formal*

ihn
him

bitte
please

an
to

eine
a

Partei
political party, Partei

Das
The

Leben
Life

an
at

Bord
board

eines
of a

Schiffes
ship

ist
is

geprägt
coined

vom
by the

Kampf
fight

mit
with

dem
the

Wetterumschwung
changing weather

Sollte
Should

man
one

beispielsweise
as an example

dazu
to it

ermuntert
encouraged

worden
were

sein
be

das
the

gesamte
whole

Leben
life

an
at

der
the

Reling
deck rail

zu
to

verbringen
spend (time)

ist
is

der
the

Wandel
change

des
of the

Wetters
weather

das
the

einzige
only

Problem
problem

das
which

man
one

selbst
oneself

bewältigen
tackle

darf
may

neben
beside

der
the

Frage
question

wer
who

die
the

Autobiographie
auto biography

schreibt
writes

und
and

wer
who

die
the

Memoiren
memoirs, reminiscences

veröffentlicht
published

„Tut
"Do (imperativ)

dies'
this

zu
to

meinem
my

Gedächtnis"
memory"

oder
or

wie
how

man
one

auf
in

neudeutsch
new german

sagen
say

kann
can

„wenn
"if

du
you

das
that, this

machst,
do,

dann
then

denk'
think (imperativ)

wenigstens
at least

an
at, to, 'of'

mich
me

Ich
I

habe
have

gerne
gladly

nichts
nothing

mit
with

der
the

alten
old

Sprache
language

zu
to

tun
do

aber
but

bin
am

froh
glad

dass
that

ich
I

sie
them

kennenlernen
to get to know

durfte
mayed, were allowed to

Insofern
in so far

ist
is

die
the

Frage
question

nach
of, about

der
the

richtigen
right

Kirche
church

eng
tightly

verknüpft
associated, linked

mit
with

dem
the

Umstand
circumstance

der
of the

Wirtschaftsgemeinschaft
economic community

in
in

der
which

man
one

sich
oneself

befindet
finds

Kein
No

Kapitän
captain

der
on the

Welt
world

würde
would

einen
a

Bahai
Bahai

an's
to the

Funkgerät
radio device

lassen
let

Nur
Only

der
the

neueste
newest

Funkspruch
radiogram, radio message

wäre
would be

dann
then

relevant
relevant

Neunzehnte
nineteenth

Zäsur
turning point

Wählen
choose

Sie
you

Korintha
[name]

Geringa-Geringcko
[name]-[name]

An
At

Bord
Board

sind
are

alle
all

religiös
religious

außer
except

dem
the

Kapitän
captain

der
the

Gallionsfigur
Figurehead

den
the

Matrosen
sailors

den
the

Gästen
guests

den
the

Mitarbeitenden
employees

und
and

dem
the

Spiegelbild
mirror image, image in the mirror

auf
on

der
the

anderen
other

Seite
side

der
of the

Reling
deck rail

Deshalb
This is why, therefor

gehen
go, walk

die
the

Offiziere
officers

oft
often

gemeinsam
together

mit
with

der
the

falschen
wrong

Passagierin
passenger

in
in, into

die
the

Kapelle
chapel

um
in order, for to

zu
to

beten
pray

»Neptun,
Neptune

oh
oh

Neptun
neptun

gib'
giv

den
the

blinden
blind

OffizierInnen
officers, gendered

die
the

Kraft
power

endlich
finally

in
in

den
the

Maschinenraum
machine room

zu
to

finden«
find

heißt
to be called a name, here: is being usually said

es
it

dann
then

oft
often

und
and

»manche
some

gehen
go

nur
only

heimlich
secretly

dort
there

hin«
there

Zwanzigste
twentiest

Zäsur
turning point

Man
one

kann
can

sich
oneself

auch
too

auf
on

ein
a

Thema
topic

fokussieren
focus.

An
a

Bord
board

der
of the

MS
ms

daneben
beside

glauben
believe

alle
all

an
in

zwei
two

Probleme
problems

den
the

Wetterumschwung
weather change

den
the

Turmbau
tower building

zu
to /in/of

Babel
babel

Zwar
right so

waren
were

zeitweise
during a phase

zahlreiche
numerous

Baumaterialien
construction materials

gebunkert
bunkered

und
and

auf
on

den
the

Laufflächen
walking surface, area, way

der
of the

Kombüse
caboose

zwischengelagert
stored intermediately

worden
were

aber
but

es
it

fehlte
missed

noch
still

die
the

passende
matching, corresponding

Baugenehmigung
authroization to construct, build

Deshalb
therefore

fokussierte
focussed

man
one

sich
oneself

in
in

den
the

Gesprächen
talks

auf
on

Stube
~ chamber (often in milit. Context)

in
in

der
the

Kajüte
liveable room on a ship

auf
on

der
the

Brücke
bridge

im
in the

Bordradio
board radio

und
and

am
at the

Pool
pool

auf
on, for

den
the

Wetterumschwung
weather change

Ich
I

glaube
believe

dass
that

heute
today

das
the

gute
good

Wetter
weather

von
from

Backbord
Larboard

nach
to

Steuerbord
starboard

wechselt
changes

und
and

gestern
yesterday

achtern
aft

war
was

das
the

Wetter
weather

so
so

schön
good

da
then, thus, so

bin
am

ich
I

ihm
him

hinterhergereist
to travel the same way as
someone else

Sie
you, *formal*

auch
too

hier
here

im
in the

Maschinenraum
engine room

einundzwanzigste
twentyfirst

Zäsur
turning point

keine Angaben
no ~ admissions, formal
information

das
that

ist
is

aber
but

auch
also

ein
a

ruhiger
silent

Dienstag
thursday

Hier
Here

an
at

Bord
board

der
of the

MS
MS

daneben
beside

ist
is

das
the

Wirtschaftsgefüge
economic arrangement

recht
quite

einfach
easy, simple, single, ordinary

strukturiert
structured

Alle
All

relevanten
relevant

Änderungen
Changes

werden
are being

an
at, to

die
the

Brücke
bridge

kommuniziert
communicated

dafür
therefor, for this

wurden
were

Telefonleitungen
phone lines

verlegt
installed, placed

aber
but

auch
as well

ein
a

Bordeigenes
bord-own

Netzwerk
network

für
for

Telekommunikationsgeräte
telecommunication devices

errichtet
built-up, installed

die
which

audiovisuelle
audivisual

Materialien
materials

transportieren
transport

können
can

aber
but

auch
as well, too

Text
text

Von
From

der
the

Reling
deck rail

aus
>from

kann
can

ich
I

das
the

Netzwerk
network

nur
only

beobachten
observe

wenn
when

es
it

über
using, throug, per

Funk
radio

betrieben
run, practised, prosecuted, pursued

wird
is being

Dafür
Therefor

habe
have

ich
I

eine
a

Antenne
antenna

an
at

mein
my

Sektglas
sparkling wine glas

angeklebt
to clue to, attatch

das
which

ich
I

nur
only

dafür
for that

aus
out of

meiner
my

Unterhose
underwear

entnahm
to take out

nun
now

kann
can

ich
I

ein
a

Ohr
ear

an
at

das
the

Sektglas
sparkling wine glass

halten
hold

und
and

mir
me, to me

werden
are being

alle
all

Inhalte
contents

diktiert
dictated, (named)

die
which

die
the

Antenne
antenna

erhält
receives

Für
For

alle
all

anderen
other

Inhalte
contents

die
which

per
per, using

Kabel
cable

transportiert
transported

werdenden
in the state of being, beinglyish

muss
must

ich
I

ein
a

Kabel
cable

im
in the

zentralen
central

Rechengerät
calculating device

einstecken
plug in

Dort
There

werden
are being

wie
how, just like

bei
with

der
the

Post
post

Nachrichten
messages

an
to

die
the

Adressaten	adressees, receivers
weitergeleitet	forwarded, passed through
Alle	All
Teilnehmer	participants
am	at the
bordeigenen	board own
Netzwerk	network
melden	register
sich	oneself
morgens	in the morning
bei	during, at
dem	the
Rechner	calculator
an	>> register, *sich anmelden*
nennen	name
ihren	their
Namen	names
und	and
ihre	their
Position	position
Unterdeck/Deck/Brücke	under deck, deck, bridge
Außenbordbuchse	outboard-plug
Ebene	level
etc.	and so on.
bis	until
Radargerät	radio device
Backbord	larboard
Steuerbord	starboard
Mittig	central
Achtern	aft
Gallionsfigurrichtung	figurehead
Zimmernummer	room number
Rang	range
Einmal	once
habe	have
ich	I
so	to pretend (so tun)
getan	did like, pretended
als	as
sei	would be
ich	I
der	the
Zentralrechner	central calculating device
da	there
hat	has
sich	itself
der	the
Kapitän	captain
bei	at, near, relyingly to
mir	me
angemeldet	signed in
als	as
Brücke: +5:Steuerbord:Gallionsfigurric htung:Kap	bridge: +5:starboard:figurehead:cpt
Kapitän **captain**	
Wenn	If
mich	to me, in reference to me
der	the
Zentralrechner	central calculator
seither	since

fragt
asks

wer
who

ich
I

sei
would be

antworte
answer

ich
I

meist
in most of the cases, mostly, often, usually

nur
only

noch
still

„Reling"
"deck rail"

die
the

Beschwerden
troubles, afflictions

halten
hold

sich
themselves

in
in

Grenzen..
borders

Wenn
When

also
so, concluding, indicating a rule here

der
the

Maschinenraum
machine room

mitteilt
informs, tells, states to a specific person; „*messages*"

dass
that

der
the

Kapitän
captain

durchsagen
announce

soll
shall

dass
that

bitte
please

Fahrgäste
passengers

mit
with

ihren
their

Sektgläsern
sparkling wine glasses

eintreffen
arrive

sollen
shall

die
the

Zylinder
cylinders

leerzuschippen
to shovel empty

muss
must

der
the

Maschinenraum
machine room

folgenden
following, the following

Text
text

an
to the

den
the

Zentralrechner
central calculating central

schicken
send

Unterdeck:-5
under deck:-5

bis
until, up to

-3:Mittig:Achtern:M
-3:intermediate:aft:M

Kapitän
captain

Zylinder
cylinder

laufen
run, get filled

voll
full

bitte
please

Fahrgästinnen
passengers, gendered

informieren
inform

Maschinenraum
machine room

Der
The

Zentralrechner
central calculater

schaut
looks up

dann
then

in
in

der
the

Liste
list

der
of the

morgendlichen
morningly

Anmeldungen
registrations

nach
nachschauen – to look up

welche
which

Adresse
adress

der
the

Kapitän
captain

angegeben
indicated, stated

hat
has

»Brücke:
+5:Steuerbord:Gallionsfigurric
htung:Kap«
bridge:
+5:starboard:figurehead:cpt

und
and

schickt
sends

dann
then

Unterdeck:-5
under deck

bis
until, up to

-3:Mittig:Achtern:M
-3:intermediate/central:aft:M

»Zylinder
cylinders

laufen
run, get filled

voll
full

bitte
please

FahrgästInnen
passengers, gendered

informieren«
inform

Maschinenraum
machine room

an
to

Brücke:
+5:Steuerbord:Gallionsfigurric
htung:Kap
bridge:
+5:starboard:figurehead:cpt

Der
The

Kapitän
captain

kann
can

dann
then

wiederum
again

mit
with

Brücke:
+5:Steuerbord:Gallionsfigurric
htung:Kap
bridge:
+5:starboard:figurehead:cpt

Maschinenraum
machine room, engine room

Durchsage
announcement

erfolgt
occurred, took place, was
carried out
|
captain

Kapitän
captain

antworten
answer

woraufhin
whereupon

der
the

Zentralrechner
central calculating device

an
at the, to

den
the

Maschinenraum
engine room

mitteilt
conveys, discloses, tells,
informs, *messages*

dass
that

Unterdeck:-5
under deck: -5

bis
until

-3:Mittig:Achtern:M
-3:central:aft:M

»Durchsage
Announcement

erfolgt«
happenned, occurred, was conducted

Kapitän
captain

Da
As

mit
with

der
the

Zeit
time

der
the

Zentralrechner
central calculator

immer
always, consecutively, steadily

mehr
more

in
in

Vergessenheit
oblivion, forgottenness

geriet
to get into

wurde
was

ein
a

neues
new

Protokoll
protocol

entwickelt
developped

das
which

erlaubt
allows

dem
to the

Zentralrechner
central calculator

mitzuteilen
to to inform

an
to

wen
whom

man
one

beabsichtigt
intends

eine
a

Nachricht
message

zu
to

senden
send

und
and

der
which

zurücksendet
sends back

wie
like, just like, *comparative*

diejenige
theese, named person, *the person referred to before*

Person
person

zu
to

erreichen
reach

ist
is

Die
The

eigentliche
actual, proper, underlying

Nachricht
message

wird
is being

dann
then

über
over

kleinere
smaller

Zentralrechner
sentral calculators

weitergegeben
forwarded

die
which

die
the

Routenbeschreibung
roude description

vom
from the

Zentralrechner
central calculator

dazubekommen
to get additionally

Dadurch
Due to this, through this, as a result

konnte	**eine**	**und**
could, were able to	a	and
der	**dritte**	**SteinCoin**
the	third	[name]
Zentralrechner	**Tätigkeit**	**EiCoin**
central calculator	activity	[name]
endlich	**aufnehmen**	**WaiCoin**
finally	to take up, *here: to start*	[name]
auch	**Seither**	**und**
too	Since then	[name]
Dialektiker	**berechnet**	**LafonCoin**
dialectician	calculates	[name]
werden	**der**	**Stoltencoin**
become	the	[name]
und	**große**	**LahnCoin**
and	grand, big	[name]
neben	**Zentralrechner**	**MattCoin**
besides	central calculator	[name]
der	**auch**	**ApCoin**
the	as well	[name]
Registratur	**die**	**Schmoin**
registry	the	[name]
der	**bordeigenen**	**Coiller**
of the	board own	[name]
Teilnehmenden	**Währungen**	**&**
participants	currencies	&
und	**LinnRCoin**	**Coiller**
and	[name]	[name]
den	**SchoCoin**	**StrauN**
the	[name]	[name]
Verbindungen	**(nur**	**SchmüCoin**
connections	only	[name]
zwischen	**für**	**DahlCoin**
between	for	[name]
den	**Schokoladeneise),**	**Stakoin**
the	chocolate ice creams	[name]
kleinen	**AltMünz**	**Etzcoin**
small	[name]	[name]
Zentralrechnern	**CoinLe**	**und**
central calculators	[name]	and

ScheeKoin
[name]; *see list of financial ministers of germany*

Die
The

elektrischen
electric

Währungen
currencies

wurden
were

alle
all

in
in

Ordner
folders

eingeteilt
indexed, graded, graduated, disposed

die
the

auf
on

eigenen
own

Festplatten
memories

gespeichert
saved

waren
were

und
and

permanent
permanently

Unterordner
sub-folders

anlegten
created, set

wenn
if

auch
also

nur
only

eine
one

Mitteilung
message

die
the

über
over

den
the

Zentralrechner
central calculator

lief
went

sie
them

betraf
concerned

Da
as

der
the

Zentralrechner
central calculator

durch
through this

die
which

nur
only

0,1
0.1

Promille
per mill, per thousand

Tantiemen
share in profits

pro
per

Transaktion
transaction

auch
also

gar
even

keine
no

finanziellen
financial

Sorgen
sorrows

mehr
any more

hatte
had

wurde
were

darüberhinaus
moreover, furthermore

ein
a

Sprachprogramm
speech program, language program

entwickelt
developped

das
which

erlaubt
allows

dem
to the

Zentralrechner
central calculator

Fragen
Questions

zu
to

stellen
pose

wie
how

„Sind
are

Ihre
your

Antworten
answers

rechtssicher?"
secure regardings laws

„Darf
May

ich
I

Ihre
Your

Antworten
answers

lesen?"
read

„Kann
can

ich
I

Sie
you, *formal*

ein
a

Buch
book

schreiben
write

lassen
let

und
and

so
as, like

tun
do

als
as

sei
would be

es
it

meines?"
mine

„Darf
May

ich
I

Sie
you

abschalten?"
to turn off

„Sind
Are

Sie
you, *formal*

in
in

der
the

Lage,
position, situation, status

den
the

Kurs
course (route)

des
of the

Schiffes
ship

zu
to

berechnen?"
calculate

Spätestens
not later than, at the latest

bei
during

der
the

letzten
last

Frage
question

ist
is

der
the

Zentralrechner
central calculator

auf
on

die
the

Eingaben
entries

seiner
of his

Sensoren
sensors

angewiesen
depending, reliant

oder
or

muss
must

auf
on

die
the

Begrenzheit
boundedness, narrowness, 'in borders'

seiner
of his

Datenbank
data base

hinweisen
indicate

Ist
Is

kein
no

Kompass
compass

an
at

den
the

Bordrechner
bord calculator

angeschlossen
attatched, connected

und
and

ist
is

dem
the

Zentralrechner
central calculator

nicht
not

bekannt
known

in
in

welchem
which

Verhältnis
ratio

der
this on, (he), it

räumlich
spacially

zum
to the

Schiff
ship

steht
stands

kann
can

auch
as well, too, 'thus'

die
the

Subtraktion
substraction

nicht
not

stattfinden
to take place

Von
Of

der
the

magnetischen
magnetic

Abweichung
deviation, aberration

des
of the

Schiffes
ship

und
and

des
of the

Planeten
planet

einmal
once

abgesehen
exempting, to look away, to exculde regarding a consideration

„Haben
Have

Sie
you, *formal*

sich
yourself

schon
already

einmal
once

selbst
youself

beobachtet
observed

Maschine?"
machine?

müsste
would must

jede
every

künstliche
artificial

Intelligenz
intelligence

sprengen
burst, detonate

Seitdem
Since then

im
in the

Jahre
year

2020
2020

die
the

Rohrpost
letter shoot, pneumatic delivery, chute

und
and

die
the

Kommunikation
communication

über
using

Röhren
pipes

wieder
again

beschlossen
decided

wurde
was

mussten
musted, had to

zahlreiche
in large number, countrich

Änderungen
Changes

am
an the

Schiffskörper
ships body, hull

vorgenommen
conducted, carry out

werden
to be, become

Währenddessen
During this

hatte
had

ich
I

die
the

ganze
whole

Zeit
time

an
at

der
the

Reling
deck rail

zu
to

stehen
stand

Wände
walls

und
and

Decken
ceilings

wurden
were

quer
cross

durch
through

den
the

Schiffskörper
ships hull, underwater part, to whole swimming construction

aufgerissen
to tear open

damit
such that

Röhren
pipes

mit
with

kurzer
short

Strecke
distance, route

und
and

wenigen
few

Biegungen
bends, curves

von
from

der
the

Brücke
bridge

zum
to the

Maschinenraum
engine room

gelegt
to lay down

werden
could

konnten
and

und
and

ein
a

Raum
room

für
for

die
the

Verteilung
distribution

von
of

Rohrpost
chute, letter shoot, pneumatic post

wurde
was

direkt
directly

unterhalb
below

der
the

Brücke
bridge

eingefügt
inserted

weshalb
why

die
the

Brücke
bridge

um
at the value of

2,50
2.50

Meter
meters

angehoben
raised, lifted

werden
to be, become

musste
musted, had to

Dafür
For this

wurde
was

ein
a

Nachbarschiff
neighbour ship

angetäut
fixed using ropes

auf
on

dem
which

eine
a

riesige
huge

Versammlung
assembly

stattfand
to take place

die
which

vom
off the

illegalen
illegal

Behelfszugang
remedy access

„Strickleiter
rope ladder

zur
to the

Brücke"
bridge

ablenkte
deviated

während
while

ein
a

Kran
crane

jene
those

und
and

die
the

Brücke
bridge

selbst
itself

anhob
rose, lifted

Beinahe
almost

hätte
had

ein
a

Schlepper
tugboat

das
the

angetäute
fixed using ropes

Schiff
ship

weggeschleppt
to drag off

und
and

so
thus

die
the

unrechtmäßige
unrighteous

Aktion
action

offenbart
revealed

aber
but

ein
a

befreundeter
friends with

Tanker
tankship

wies
indicated

auf
(on); *auf etwas hinweisen: to indicate ~towards, that*

auslaufendes
running out, leaking

Öl
oil

hin
>indicate

weshalb
why

der
the

Schlepper
tugboat

schließlich
finally

selbst
itself

antäute
attatch using ropes

und
and

so
thus

eine
a

illustre
illustrious

Reihe
row

von
of

drei
three

Booten
boats

im
in the

Hafen
harbour

lag
laid

Seitdem
Since then

die
the

Rohrpostzentrale
shooting post central, chute central, pneumatic post- , letter shoot central

fertig
finished

ist
is

werden
are

beständig
steadily

unzustellbare
undelivereable

Rohrpost-Mitteilungen
letter shoot - messages

von
off

Bord
board

geschleudert
thrown

nämlich
namely

durch
through

ein
a

Rohr
pipe

mit
with

einem
a

offenen
open

Ende
end

das
which

in
in

dem
the

Verteilungs-Raum
distribution room

in
in

der
the

„Normalverteilungs-Ecke
gaussian distribution corner

nach
according to

C.F.
Carl Friedrich

Gauss
Gauss 10 DM + 20 Sh +

in
in

Form
shape

eines
of a

großen
huge, big

Trichters
funnel, cone

erreichbar
reacheable

ist
is

Die
the

Verteiler
distributors

müssen
have to

unzustellbare
undeliverable

Nachrichten
messages

einfach
simply

nur
only

in
in

den
the

großen
big

Trichter
cone

werfen
throw

Die
The

„Unzustellbaren"
Undeliverables

landen
land

dann
then

in
in

einer
a

Art
kind of

Schleuse
air lock

in
in

der
which

ein
a

Überdruck
overpressure

aufgebaut
established

wird
is being

der
which

diese
theese

dann
then

mit
with

einer
a

gewissen
certain

Energie
energy

von
off

Bord
board

schleudert
throws, catapults, slingshoots

Die
The

angetäute
attached using ropes

MS
MS

Volltreffer
'full hit', direct hit, bull's eye,
but in serious manner, too

hat
has

so
like this

bereits
already

eine
a

beträchtliche
considerable

Beule
bulge, bump

in
in

der
the

Bordwand
board wall

entwickelt
developped

das
which

dahinter	der	aber
behind	the	but
liegende	**Reling**	**führt**
lying	deck rail	guides
Schiff	**der**	**eine**
ship	the	a
ein	**Kapitän**	**kleine**
a	captain	small
kleiner	**selbst**	**stählerne**
small	himself	iron
Schlepper	**steht**	**Vorrichtung**
tugship	stands	mechanism, equipment
aus	**auf**	**durch**
from	on	through, by
der	**der**	**dessen**
the	the	their
Nachkriegszeit	**anderen**	**Ärmel**
post war era	other	sleeve
ist	**Seite**	**entlang**
is	side	along
davon	**der**	**des**
from this	of the	of the
noch	**Reling**	**Oberkörpers**
still	deck rail	upper part of the body, torso
unbeeindruckt	**und**	**zu**
unimpressed	and	to
dort	**scheint**	**einer**
there	appears	a
stehen	**sich**	**kleinen**
stand	himself	small
noch	**nur**	**Plattform**
still	only	platform
immer	**an**	**auf**
always	at, near	on
alle	**ihr**	**der**
all	her	the
Passagiere	**festzuhalten**	**er**
passengers	to hold on	he
an	**tatsächlich**	**steht**
at	indeed, as a fact	stands

Seite | page 93

Deshalb Therefor	**Bordwände** board walls, ship walls	**und** and
reist travels	**und** and	**den** the
jener thes, named	**sämtliche** all	**Schlepper** tugboat
Kapitän captains	**Inneneinrichtungen** interiour furniture	**zum** to the
nur only	**und** and	**Ablegen** departure, *to unfix a ship and drive/sail away*
sehr very	**Kabinenwände** cabin walls	**bringen** bring, *in the sense of to make someone [to unfix the ship from pier]*
wenig few	**durchschlagen** punch through	
Die The	**Erst** First	**Es** It
Unzustellbaren undeliverables	**dann** then	**wird** is being
müssten would must	**könnten** could	**gemutmaßt** speculated
um in order to	**die** the	**dass** that
die the	**in** in	**der** the
Party celebration	**den** the	**Schlepper** tugboat
auf on	**großen** big	**den** the
jenem named	**roten** red	**ganzen** whole
Schiff ship	**Trichter** funnel, cone	**Hafen** harbour
aufzulösen to dissolve, resolve	**geworfenen** thrown	**bewegen** move
zuerst first	**Mitteilungen** messages	**kann** can
beide both	**dort** there	**aber** but
	angelangen arrive	**das** that

sind
are

unbestätigte
unconfirmed

Gerüchte
rumours

aus
from

der
the

Zeit
time

in
in

der
which

ein
a

Sozialdemokrat
social democrat

Kapitän
captain

war
was

Aktuell
currently

ist
is

ein
a

Nachfahre
successor, descendant
(context family)

von
of

„Hulk"
"hulk"

Kapitän
captain

der
who

zuerst
first

den
the

Timmothee-und-Strumpf-Kapitän
Timmothee-and-sock-captain

von
over

Bord
board

gejagt
chased

hatte
had

und
and

dann
then

erläuterte
explicated

dass
that

‚Hulk'
'Hulk'

eine
a

grazile
gracile

Frau
Woman

geheiratet
married

hatte
had

die
which

seine
his

Urgroßmutter
grand-grandmother

zur
to the

Welt
world

brachte
brought

Diese
This

sei
would be

ganz
completely

rot
red

gewesen
been

weshalb
which is why

die
the

grüne
green

Farbe
colour

aufwändig
elaborate, costly, complex

über
over, in the sense of 'using'

Sonnenbäder
sun bathings

zurückgeholt
to get back, bring back

werden
being

musste
had to

Das
The

blau
blue

der
of the

Uniform
uniform

passte
matched

nicht
not

zum
to the

grün
green

auf
on

der
the

Haut
skin

also
so, thus, indicating a conclusion

nahm
took

ich
I

dem
from the. off the, of the

Kapitän
captain

seine
his

Uniform
uniform

weg
away

und
and

verschenkte
made as a present

sie
it

einem
to a

unkreativen
uncreative

Franzosen
french man

mit
with

deutschem
german

Pass
passport

Seither
Since then

legt
departs

das
the

Schiff
ship

zwar
indeed, as indicator for a rather negative situation

permanent
permanently

ab
>departure: ablegen

aber
but

ich
I

fühle
feel

mich
myself

dadurch
through this, due to this, as an implication of this

nicht
not

mehr
any more

so
so, that much

einsam,
lonely

an
at

der
the

Reling
deck rail

da
there

fiel
fell (catched my eye)

mir
to me

auf
auffallen > catch an eye

dass
that

der
the

Hafen
harbour

in
in

dem
which

mein
my

Schiff
ship

liegt
lies

der
the

Pool
pool

eines
of a

größeren
bigger

Kreuzfahrtschiffes
cruise ship

ist
is

an
at

dessen
'whiches'

Reling
deck rail

womöglich
potentially

jemand
someone

gestanden
stood

hatte
had

von
of

dem
whom

ich
I

niemals
never

erfahren
learn, to get to know

würde
would

Ich
I

beschloss
decided

mehr
more

Informationen
information

von
of

dem
the

Schlepper
tugboat

zu
to

erfragen
demand

der
which

den
the

ganzen
whole

Hafen
port

bewegen
move

konnte
could

und
and

verblieb
remained

zunächst
then, first, as one of the next
events

an
at

der
the

Reling
deck rail

stehend
standing

Zweiundzwanzigste
twentyfirst

Zäsur
zaesoor

Bücher
Books

müssen
must

nicht
not

mehr
any more

gedruckt
printed

werden
to be

Die
The

Bücher
books

die
which

an
at

Bord
board

gedruckt
printed

werden
are being

werden
were

alle
all

über
using, per

den
the

Zentralrechner
central calculator

verschickt
sent

Soll
Should

ein
a

Buch
book

gedruckt
printed

werden
to be

wird
is

das
the

Buch
book

und
and

der
the

Empfänger
recipient

in
into

die
the

Buchdruckkombüse
book printing caboose

gesendet
sent

wo
where

dann
then

der
the

Druck
pressure; print

stattfindet
taketh place

Wird
Is

ein
a

Buch
book

nicht
not

gedruckt
printed

kann
can

es
it

auch
also, as well

als
as

Text
text

an
to

den
the

Empfänger
recipient

geschickt
sent

werden
to be

der
which

es
it

dann
then

entweder
either

selbst
itself

ausdruckt
prints

oder
or

damit
with it

zur
to the

Buchdruckkombüse
book printing caboose

läuft
walks

aber
but

manche
some

lesen
read

den
the

Text
text

auch
also, as well

direkt
directly

wie
how

vom
from the

Zentralrechner
central calculator

zugesendet
sent'

Wo
Where

die
the

Bücher
books

herkommen
come from

die
which

man
one

auf
on

die
the

eine
one

oder
or

andere
other

Weise
manner

lesen
read

kann
can

ist
is

den
the

meisten
most

egal.
equal, doesn't matter

Durch
Through

die
the

an
at

die
the

Buchdruckkombüse
book printing caboose

angeschlossene
attached

Papierrecyclinganlage
paper recycling facility

kann
can

Papier
paper

relativ
relatively

günstig
cheap

bezogen
to order, draw, but without negotiations

werden
to be, being

aber
but

Tinten
inks

müssen
must

aus
from

der
the

Portokasse
petty cash

des
of the

Kapitäns
captain

bezahlt
paid

und
and

deshalb
therefore

förmlich
formally

und
and

höflich
politely

beantragt
requested

werden
be, become

Deshalb
Therefore

haben
have

sich
themselves

viele
many

die
who

sich
themselves

am
at the

Zentralrechner
central calculator

anmelden
to sign in

können
can

dazu
to it

entschieden
decide

einfach
easily

die
the

Texte
texts

direkt
directly

auf
on

ihrer
their

Mitteilungsanzeige
message display, monitor

zu
to

lesen
read

Jemand
Someone

hat
has

sogar
even

ein
a

eigenes
own

Gerät
device

erfunden
invented

mithilfe
with help of

dessen
which

er
he

Texte
texts

anzeigen
to display, show

kann
can

und
and

hat
has

es
it

an
to

alle
all

Kombüsen
cabooses

verkauft
sold

die
which

schon
already

ihren
their

Sand
sand

aus
from

der
the

Fußmatte
doormat, foot mat

geschüttelt
shaked

hatten
had

manche
some

haben
have

aber
but

auch
also, too

ein
a

solches
such

Gerät
device

überreicht
handed over

bekommen
received

obwohl
even if

sie
they

noch
still

Sand
sand

in
in

der
the

Fußmatte
foot mat

hatten
had

Weil
Because
es
it

als
as

„schiffsdienlich"
serving to the ship

gilt
weighed, assigned

dem
(from) the

Kapitän
captain

keine
captain

Tinte
ink

abzunötigen
extort, withdraw

gelten
one says so, rumourous,
'apply'

gedruckte
printed

Bücher
books

als
as

weniger
less

gut
good

nur
only

die
the

elektrische
electric

Version
version

auf
on

den
the

blinkenden
blinking

oder
or

nichtblinkenden
notblinking

eckigen
angled, angular, squared

Kästchen
casket

mit
with

beweglichen
movable

Punkten
points

gelten
are said to be

als
as

gerecht
just

Deshalb
Therefor

sind
are

viele
many

Passagiere
passengers

mit
with

Blinkstein
blinking Stone

zu
to
RichterInnen
Judges, *gendered*

geworden
become

und
and

verurteilen
judged

alle
all

die
who

ein
a

Buch
book

bei
with

sich
themselves

tragen
carry

obwohl
even if

sie
they

das
that

nicht
not

dürfen
may

Die
The

Brücke
bridge

wurde
was

darüber
about this
nicht
not

informiert
informed

sondern
but

es
it

wurden
were

kleine
small

mit
with

Elektroschockern
electronic shock gun

ausgestattete
equipped

Gegenoffizier-Gruppen
counter-officer-groups

geformt
formed

die
which

durch
through

die
the

Bordwände
board walls, ship walls

oberhalb
above

des
the

Maschinenraums
engine room

hindurchgehen
to walk through

können
can
und
and

sich
themselves

deshalb
therefor

wie
how

selbstverständlich
naturally, of course

auf
on

der
the

Brücke
bridge

aufhalten
to spend time

Viele
just like

andere
other

Schiffe
ships

im
in the

Hafen
harbour

haben
have

sich
themselves

das
that

zu
to

eigen
own

gemacht
made
und
and

selbst
even, themselves, self

solche
such

Gruppen
groups

auf
on

die
the

Brücke
bridge

der
of the

MS
ms

daneben
besides

geschickt
sent

Deshalb
therefor

ist	**von**	**durch**
is	from	through
die	**allen**	**Bordwände**
the	all	board walls
Brücke	**die**	**gehen**
bridge	who	walk
zwar	**nicht**	**können**
indeed	not	can
einerseits	**auf**	**aber**
on the one hand	on	but
wegen	**die**	**trotzdem**
because of	the	anyways
Überfüllung	**Brücke**	**auf**
over filling	bridge	on
geschlossen	**gehen**	**der**
closed	walk	the
und	**können**	**Brücke**
and	can	bridge
andererseits	**oder**	**stehen**
on the other hand	or	stand
der	**aufgrund**	**einseitig**
the	due to	one-sidedly
interessanteste	**von**	**mit**
most interesting	of	with
Ort	**Umständen**	**Anfragen**
place	circumstances	requests
an	**die**	**belastet**
at	which	stressed
Bord	**dazu**	**ohne**
board.	to it	without
Der	**führten**	**dass**
The	led, lead	that
Zentralrechner	**dass**	**die**
central calculator	that	the
hingegen	**sie**	**Rechenkapazität**
however	they	calculating capacity
wird	**zwar**	**dauerhaft**
is	~ if not	long lastingnot provisional
seither	**nicht**	**erhöht**
since then	not	raised

worden
be

wäre
was

Einmal
Once

gesellte
joined, to become friendly part of a group, *from Geselle: companion, a person who learns a handraft*

sich
himself

ein
a

osmanischer
osmanic, turkish
Zuckerbäcker
sugar baker

zum
to the

Zentralrechner
central calculator

und
and

belegte
occupied

einen
a

Teil
part

des
of the

Arbeitsspeichers
random access memory (provisory memory for calculations)

beständig
steadily

abwechselnd
alternatingly

mit
with

Null
zero

und
and

Eins
one

während
while

gleichzeitig
at the same time

die
the

Festplatte
memory

von
off

Viren
virusses

befreit
freed, set free; here: cleaned, cleared

und
and

die
the

Anfragen
requests

kurzzeitig
on short terms

durch
(by)

Fahrstuhlmusik
music that is being played in elevators

unterbrochen
interrupted

wurden
were

aber
but

mit
with

dem
the

Wechsel
change

des
of the

Verwaltungsrats
administration council

der
of the

Reederei
ship owning company

wurde
was

der
the

Zentralrechner
central calculator

auf
on, to

Auslieferungszustand
delivery state

zurückgesetzt
set' back

und
and

da
as

er
he

angeblich
alledgedly

wie
how

man
one

auf
on

der
the

Brücke
bridge

vernehmen
to perceive, hear

könne
could, *subj.*

dem
to the, the

Ansehen
reputation

der
of the

MS
MS

daneben
besides

schade
damaging

von
of

der
the

Notstromversorgung
emergency currency supply,
emergency energy supply

getrennt
seperated

Seitdem
Since then

ist
is

das
the

Schicksal
destiny

vom
of the

Zentralrechner
central calculator

von
of

dem
the

Schiff
ship

abhängig
dependant

für
for

das
which

er
he

Mitteilungen
messages

verteilt
spready

Glücklicherweise
fortunately

war
was

nach
after

dem
the

Wechsel
change

des
of the

Verwaltungsrats
administration council

ein
a

falscher
wrong

Kapitän
captain

auf
on

der
the

Brücke
bridge

erschienen
appeared

und
and

hat
has

begonnen
begun

die
the

Konsense
consensusses

der
of the

Brücken-Bewohner
bridge-inhabitants

manche
some

haben
have

sich
themselves

ein
a

Penthouse
penthouse

eingerichtet
furnished

um
in order to

einen
a

kürzeren
shorter

Weg
way

zur
to the

Arbeit
work

zu
to

haben
have

zusammenzufassen
concluding

Da
as
die
the

„Brückianer",
bridgiander

wie
how

sie
they

andernorts
elsewhere

auf
on

dem
the

Schiff
ship

getauft
baptemized

wurden
were

sich
themselves

gerne
likely

gegenseitig
mutually

imitierten
imitated

war
was

so
like this

die
the

Zusammenfassung
conclusion, summary

des
of the

falschen
wrong

Kapitäns
captain

immer
steadily

mehr
more

zum
to

Konsens
consensus

geworden
became

Sobald
As soon as

also
thus

die
the

Penthouses
penthouses

zurückgebaut
built back

und
and

die
the

durch
through

Bordwände
board walls, ship walls

gehen
walk

könnenden
canning, to be able to

Gegenoffiziere
counter-officers

von
of
der
the

Brücke
bridge

entfernt
seperated

oder
or

in
in

den
the

Regelbetrieb
regular mode od operation,
regular hustle'n'bustle

integriert
integrated

waren
were

beides
both

ist
is

möglich
possible

war
was

der
the

falsche
wrong

Kapitän
captain

in
in

der
the

Lage
position

statt
instead

einer
of a

Zusammenfassung
summary

einen
an

Befehl
order

zu
to

äußern
utter

„Super"
"Super", "Great!",

sagte
said

ich
I

zum
to the

irischen
irish

Reiseleiter
travel guide

der
who

eine
a

gregoreanische
gregorian

Männergesangsgruppe
male singing group

aus
from

dem
the

Vatikan
vatican
über
over

die
the

Reling
deck rail

führte
guided

ich
I

muss
must

nur
only

noch
still

den
the

richtigen
right

Kapitän
captain

finden
find

und
and

unter
under

einem
a

Vorwand
false pretenses

in
in

den
the

Ruhestand
retirement

versetzen
replace
Oh
oh

oh
oh

ok
ok

we're
wir

going
gehen

to
zu

a
einer

bar
Bar, Kneipe

d'you
tust du (childish)

come
kommen

with
mit

voranzugehen
to proceed, here: to walk in the front of a group

Er
He

fiel
fell

um
around

und
and

wurde
was

zertrampelt
trampled

entdeckte
discovered

einige
some

Anführungszeichen
quotation marks

die
which

die
the

Mönche
monks

fallengelassen
to let fall

hatten
had

und
and

beschloss
decided

damit
with this

endlich
finally

finnisch
finnish

zu
to

lernen
learn

Der
The

Rittergruß
ridder salute

den
which

er
he

davor
before

angedeutet
foreshadowed

hatte
had

ist
is

eine
a

mittelalterliche
middle age

Geste
gesture

die
which

früher
before

so
[to]

ähnlich
similar to

ausgeführt
conducted (executed, rather 'to go on a date', also: experiments)

worden
was

war
was

um
in order to

das
the

Visier
sight

zu
to

heben
raise

Dadurch
Through this

konnten
could

fremde
strange

Ritter
ridders, Knights

erkennen
recognize

mit
with

wem
whom

sie
they

es
it

zu
to

tun
do

hatten
had

Da
As

wir
we

beide
both

keine
no

Rüstung
armement

trugen
wore

verstand
understood

ich
I

ihn
him

nicht
not
recht
right, correctly

und
and

prostete
saluting with a drink

stattdessen
instead

mit
with

meinem
my

alkoholfreien
alcohol-free

23'er
1923

Cabernet
cabernet

Sauvignon
sauvignon

in
in

Richtung
direction

meines
of my

Spiegelbildes
mirror image

das
which

eingeschlafen
slept in

war
was

»Aufwachen!«
"Wake up"

brüllte
roared

ich
I

und
and

hoffte
hoped

dass
that

die
the

eckigen
angulous

Anführungszeichen
quotation marks

den
the

entsprechenden
corresponding

Effekt
effect

hatten
had

Stattdessen
instead

schlief
slept

ich
I

ein
(to fall asleep: einschlafen)

und
and

träumte
dreamed

von
of

einem
a

Hafen
harbour, port

in
in

unserem
our

schiffseigenen
ships own

Pool
pool

der
which

nicht
not

zu
to

finden
find

war
was

weil
because

man
one

ihn
it

genau
exactly

falsch
wrong

ausgeschildert
to put signs, sighs and so to
walls, piles and so with sighs
written, signs written on it

hatte
had

Genaugenommen
~ to be precise ~

habe
have

ich
I

selbst
myself

nie
never

den
the

Pool
pool

besucht
visited

aber
but

der
the

Hafen
harbour

den
which

ich
I

darin
in it

erträumte
to dream actively

der
that one

war
was

belebt
vivid

darin
in that

liegt
lies

ein
a

Schiff
ship

an
at
dessen
whiches

Reling
deck rail

steht
stands

ein
a

Protagonist
protagonist

eines
of a

Buches
book

und
and

ich
I

schreibe
write

auf
aufschreiben - to write 'up'

was
what

dieser
theese person

erlebt
lived

Dreiundzwanzigste
twentythird

Zäsur
zaesoor

Verschachtelungen
Interlockings (interleaving,
pyramiding, shuffling)

führen
guides

nicht
not

immer
always

zum
to the

Tod
death

Auch
Also

an
a

Bord
board

des
of the

Schiffs
ship

in
in

unserem
our

Pool
pool

war
was

ein
a

Raum
room

für
for

auf
on

See
sea

verstorbene
passed away ones

aber
but

auch
also

ein
a

Raum
room

für
for

diejenigen
those

die
who

nicht
not

an
'~in

die
the

Ereignisse
events

nach
after

dem
the

Versterben
Passing

denken
think

wollten
wanted

eine
a

Kapelle
chapel

Die
[the chapel], *The, She*

darf
may

ich
I

allerdings
although

nicht
not

aufsuchen
explore

denn
because

nur
only

eine
a

kleine
small

Bewegung
movement

konnte
could

die
the

gesamte
whole

Kapelle
chapel

zerstören
destroy

und
and

das
the

Leben
life

vieler
of many

an
a

Bord
board

des
of the

kleineren
small

Schiffs
ship

für
for

immer
ever

zerstören
destroy

Also
Thus, so, *concludingly*

hielt
held

ich
I

mich
myself

fern
far away

vom
from

unauffindbaren
unfindeable

Pool
pool

unseres
of our

Schiffes
ship

dachte
thought

aber
but

immer
always

wieder
again

an
of

die
the

Kapelle
chapel

in
in

dem
the

Schiff
ship

in
in

dessen
whiches

Pool
pool

wir
we

womöglich
potentially

vertäut
to be towed, fixed with tows

sind
are

hielte
woul l hold

ich
I

mich
myself

dort
there

auf
up (to stay somewhere: sich aufhhalten)

könnte
could

ein
a

herunterfallender
falling down

Schal
scarf

mein
my

Ende
end

sein
be

andererseits
on the other side

könnte
could

ich
I

mich
me

vermutlich
potentially

locker
easily, 'loose, casual'

im
in the

Profil
profile

eines
of a

Schuhs
shoe

entsprechender
of matching

Dimension
dimension

aufhalten
to stay somewhere, to remain somewhere

Ich
I

beschloss
decided

mich
myself

meiner
to my

direkten
direct

Umgebung
surrounding, environment
(neighbourhood)

zu
to

widmen
dedicate

und
and

fand
found

auf
on

dem
the

Boden
floor

ein
a

Buch
book

das
which

folgenden
the following

Titel
title

trug
carried, wore

»Tuch.«
"Tissue"

Vierundzwanzigste
twentyfourth

Zäsur
turning point

»Das
The

Buch«
Book

Die
The

Randbedingungen
marginal conditions

hätten
would have

wir
we

also
thus

schon
already

geklärt
cleared

dabei
whereas

sind
are

Randbedingungen
marginal conditions

oft
often

das
that

was
what

bei
here: during

Kurvendiskussionen
curve sketching (analyzing a math. function regarding its attributes)

in
in

der
the

Mathematik
maths

eher
rather

vergessen
forgotten

werden
are

Ein
A

Ich-Erzähler
First person narrator

steht
stands

an
at

der
the

Reling
deck rail

eines
of a

Schiffes
ship

Sie
You, *formal*

lesen
read

ein
a

Buch
book

Sie
you, *formal*

können
can

weiterlesen
read on

Wenn
If

die
the

Reisegruppe
travel guide

des
of the

irischen
irish

Reiseleiters
travel guide

vorbeischaut
to stop by

ist
is

das
the

meist
most

früh
early

morgens
in the morning

Die
The

TouristInnen
tourists, gendered

haben
have

dann
then

meist
mostly

einen
a

Coffee-to-go-Becher
coffee-to-go-cup

bei
with, (near)

sich
them

und
and

tragen
carry

ein
a

Tablett
tray

das
which

mit
with

einer
a

Schnur
string

um
around

den
the

Hals
neck

und
and

einem
a

Gürtel
belt

um
around

die
the

Taille
waist

befestigt
fixed, attached

ist
is

mit
with

Croissants
croissants

Brötchen
small bread things

Butter
butter

Marmelädchen
jam, (belittled)

Fondues
fondues

und
and

diversen
various

Militaria
military originating
accessoires

wie
like

Brötchen-Dolch,
small bread-dagger

Frühstücks-Haubitze,
breakfast-howitzer

Croissantabschneider
croissant-cut-off-device

oder
or

eben
even

Hühnereidekupateur
chicken-egg-cut-off-thing
(lat.)

mit
with

sich
himself

herum
around

Durch
by, using, through

einen
a

Schwerkraft-Generator
gravity-generator

unterhalb
below

jeden
every

Tablettes
tray

müssen
musted

sich
itself

die
the

TouristInnen
tourists, gendered

keinerlei
in no way

Sorgen
sorrow

um
around

ihr
their

Frühstück
breakfast

machen
make

sondern
but, rather, >instead

laufen
walk

fröhlich
happily

und
and

chaotisch
chaotically

umher
around

stoßen
push, poke

aneinander
against each other

und
and

wanken
falter, stagger, wave

dann
the

voneinander
from each other

weg
away

wobei
where, while, whereat

sie
they

meist
mostly

von
from the

der
the

anderen
other

Seite
side

her
~ from

mit
with

einem
a

weiteren
further

Touristen
tourist

einer
a

weiteren
further

Touristin
tourist, female

anstoßen
clink (glasses)

der
the

irische
irish

Reiseleiter
travel guide

hat
has

nur
only

geringfügige
insignificant

Probleme
problems

damit
with it

die
the

Menschentraube
human cluster

beieinander
~ together

zu
to

halten
hold

Manchmal
Sometimes

nehme
take

ich
I

mir
me

ein
a

Glas
glass

Orangensaft
orange juice

von
from

einem
one

der
of the

Tablette
trays

aber
but

nur
only

wenn
if

mich
me

der
the

Tourist
tourist

die
the

Touristin
tourist, female

nicht
not

beachtet
respect, follow, to be in
contact with

hat
has

Entgeisterte
aghast

Blicke
looks

bin
am

ich
I

dann
then, in these situations

gewöhnt
used to

meist
mostly

werfe
throw

ich
I

einfach
simply

das
the

Glas
glas

über
over

Bord
board

ein
a

Glas
glas

französischer
of french

Fabrikation
~production

im
in the

weiteren
further

Verlauf
course

der
of the

Seine
\His;; here: [name]

nach
towards

Paris
paris

werden
are

Glasatome
glass atoms

gewonnen
gained

immer
always

wenn
when

die
the

Seine
[name], river

zufriert
freezes to ice, leading to a
compact surface

Packeis
pack ice

wird
is being

dann
then

in
in

eine
a

Fabrik
factory

gebracht
brought

wo
where

es
it

geschmolzen
smolten

wird
is being

Das
The

entstehende
emerging

Wasser
water

wird
is being

mit
with

Stärke
starch

und
and

mehreren
multiple

Zaubersprüchen
magic hex hex sentences

in
in

Form
shape

gebracht
brought

und
and

ausschließlich
exclusively

an
to

Kreuzfahrtreedereien
cuise ship owning companies

verkauft	**nach**	**herniedergeht**
sold	towards	~ descends
Manchmal	**oben**	**Einmal**
sometimes	upwards, up, top	Once
schnappe	**fliegen**	**habe**
snap, snatch	fly	have
ich	**die**	**ich**
I	the	I
gleich	**Reling**	**ein**
directly	deck rail	a
nach	**überqueren**	**Orangensaftglas**
after	to cross	orange juice glass
dem	**wo**	**hundertfach**
the	where	a hundred tumes
Überbordwerfen	**es**	**vergrößert**
throwing over board	it	enlarged
eines	**dann**	**dafür**
of a	then	therefor
Glases	**entweder**	**musste**
glass	either	musted
besagten	**aufgefangen**	**ich**
said	catched up	I
Schwerkraftgenerator	**wird**	**nur**
gravity generator	is being	only
und	**oder**	**einem**
and	or	a
lasse	**nach**	**Passagier**
let	after	passenger
das	**Aufprall**	**die**
the	impact	the
Glas	**als**	**Kamera**
glass	as	camera
durch	**Regen**	**abnehmen**
through	rain	to take away
gezielte	**über**	**das**
targeted	over	the
Gravitationsapplikation	**der**	**Objektiv**
gravitation application	the	objective
wieder	**Schiffsoberfläche**	**abschrauben**
again	ships surface	to screw off

und
and

die
the

Kamera
camera

über
over

Bord
board

werfen
throw

Das
The

so
such

vergrößerte
enlarged

Glas
glass

habe
have

ich
I

dann
then

verwendet
used

um
in order to

eine
a

Touristin
tourist

einzufangen
to catch ('in')

eine
a

Rentnerin
retiree, female

mit
with

Regenmantel
rain coat

spielte
played

dann
then

in
in

dem
the

umgestülpten
inverted, everted, upended

Glas
glass

Kafkas
[name]

„Die
The

Verwandlung"
Metamorphosis

auf
on, to perform: aufführen

zuerst
first

widerspenstig
~ restive

aber
but

schließlich
finally

mit
with

zunehmendem
increasing

Spaß
fun

Drei
three

herbeigeeilte
came running, approached

OffizierInnen
officers, gendered

übernahmen
overtook

die
the

Rollen
roles

der
of the

Zimmersleute
timber men

alle
all

anderen
other

Rollen
roles

haben
have

wir
we

von
from

der
the

falschen
wrong

Passagierin
passenger

spielen
play

lassen
let

Der
The

Kapitän
captain

beendete
finalized, ended

das
the

Schauspiel
spectacle, play, performance
(of actors)

damals
at that time

damit
with that

das
the

Glas
glass

zu
to

Wasser
water

zu
zu

lassen
let (launch)

ignorierte
ignored

die
the

unfreiwillig
involuntarily

zusammengestellte
collocated

Theatergruppe
theatre group, group of theatre
actors

und
and

ließ
let'

sich
himself

fortan
from then on

als
as

»der
"the

große
grand

Zuwasserlass-Kapitän
to-water-let-captain

bezeichnen
designate

Selbstverständlich
of course

war
was

die
the

MS
MS

daneben
besides

in
in

den
the

polnischen
polish

Nationalfarben
national colours

gestrichen
painted

Das
That

hatte
had

den
the

einfachen
simple

Grund
reason

dass
that

das
the

Wasser
water

im
in the

Hafenbecken
harbour basin

von
of

der
the

nackten
naked

Bordwand
board wall

ferngehalten
to keep away

werden
to be, become

sollte
should

und
and

sowohl
as well

rote
red

als
as

auch
also

weiße
white

Farbe
colour

übrig
odd, remaining, left over, spare

war
was

Da
As

die
the

MS
MS

daneben
besides

unter
under

europäischer
european

Flagge
flag

zu
to

Wasser
water

gelassen
let'

worden
had been

war
was

sollte
should, *shoulded, past*

die
the

Bemalung
painting

der
of the

Bordwände
board walls

keine
no

dazu
to that

widersprüchliche
contradicting

Zuordnung
assigning, relation

zulassen
authorized

Indonesien
indonesia

Polen
poland

Georgien
georgia

die
the

Schweiz
switzerland

Österreich
austria

etc.
and so on (lat.)

wurden
were

beide
both

Farben
colors

gemischt
mixed

Da
As

ich
I

Rosa
pink

nicht
not

leiden
suffer (to like: 'to be able to suffer something)

konnte
could

die
the

Farbe
color

ist
is

vielleicht
maybe

gerade
just, minimally not yet

so
~ *almost*

im
in the

Kontext
context

Zahnabdruckmasse
teeth imprint compound

sinnvoll
meaningful

aber
but

auch
also

da
there

kann
can

man
one

fragen
ask

warum
why

man one	**anderen** other	**Optionen** options
nicht not	**Seite** side	**„Republicans"** "Republikaner"
ein a	**befohlen** ordered	**(Stier)** (bull)
Pigment pigment	**die** the	**und** and
beifügt add, attach	**Farben** colours	**„Democrats"** Demokrat
die which	**Rot** red	**(Esel)** (Esel)
jene those	**oder** or	**wobei** where at
Masse compound	**Schwarz** black	**ich** I
klar clearly	**auf** on	**mich** myself
von from the	**der** the	**aktuell** to date
Zahnfleisch gum, teethridge	**Außenwand** outer side of the wall	**meist** in the most cases
unterscheiden differentiate	**anzubringen** attach, to bring on	**für** for
lässt lets	**und** and	**Argentinisches** argentinian
Deshalb Therefore	**erhielt** received	**Rumpsteak** rump steak
habe have	**als** as	**entschied** decided
ich I	**Antwort** answer	**das** which
meinem to my	**immer** always	**der** the
Spiegelbild mirror-image	**wieder** again	**aktuelle** current
auf on	**die** the	**Papst** pope
der the	**beiden** both	**aus** ~facing

unbekannten	unknown
Gründen	reasons
und	and
auf	on
eigene	own
Initiative	initiative
hin	~ >initiative
gesegnet	blessed
hatte	had
So	This is how
kam	came
es	it
also	thus
dass	that
ich	I
der	to the
Reederei-Vertreterin,	ship owning company-agent
die	who
vorbeigeschlichen	sneaked by
war	was
einen	a
Heiratsantrag	proposal (marriage)
machte	made
und	and
dabei	during that
eine	a
Farbpalette	colour palette
leise	silently
in	in
die	the
Handtasche	handbag
manoevrierte	manoeuvered
auf	on
der	which
die	the
Farbe	colour
Rosa	pink
gänzlich	wholely
fehlte	missed
Dem	To the
vorbeikriechenden	crawling by
Kapitän	capatin
die	the
Happy	Glückliche
Hour	Stunde
hatte	had
beworben	advertised
werden	to be, become
dürfen	may
und	and
der	the
Kapitän	captain
war	was
entsprechend	correspondingly
einer	to a
Dienstanweisung	office / shift instruction
des	of the
Zentralrechners	central calculating machine
gefolgt	followed

und
and

hingegangen
went there

befahl
ordered

ich
I

schwarze
black

Farbe
colour

zu
to

bunkern
to store in a ship

und
and

rote
red

Farbe
colour

als
as

präferiertes
preferred

Gastgeschenk
guests present

anzugeben
to indicate, state, show off

Immer
Always

mehr
more

PassagierInnen
passengers, gendered

die
which

die
the

MS
MS

daneben
beside

betraten
to step onto/into

gaben
gave

statt
instead

ihrer
of their

Eintrittskarten
entry tickets

einfach
simply

direkt
directly

einen
a

Eimer
bucket

rote
red

Farbe
paint

ab
(out, to hand out, to give away: abgeben, to an authority)

So
Thus

kam
came

es
it

auch
also, as well

dass
that

die
the

MS
MS

daneben
beside

stark
strongly

überfüllt
overfilled

war
was

weshalb
why

TouristInnengruppen
tourist-groups, gendered

abwechselnd
alternatingly

über
over

Bord
board

geführt
guieded

wurden
were

Der
The

irische
irish

Reiseleiter
travel guide

hatte
had

so
like that

eine
a

Vollzeitbeschäftigung
full time occupation

gefunden
found

musste
musted

aber
but

stets
steadily

darauf
on it

achten
to take care of, to respect and consider

dass
that

keine
none

der
of the

beiden
both

Gruppen
groups

die
which

er
he

abwechselnd
alternatingly

über
over

Bord
board

führte
guided

jemals
ever

Pause
pause

machen
make

wollte
wanted

und
and

in
in

ihre
their

Kabinen
cabins

zurückkehrte
returned

Gleichzeitig
At the same time

hatte
had

er
he

ein
a

System
system

entwickelt
developped

die
the

Beschwerden
complaints

über
over

veränderte
alternated

Rahmenbedingungen
frame conditions, surrounding conditions

konsequent
consequently

und
and

friedlich
peacefully

abzuwehren
to ward, fend

indem
in, by, through

er
he

auf
on

weitere
further

zukünftige
future

Veränderungen
Changes

hinwies
indicate

Nicht
Not

nur
only

die
the

Kabinen
cabins

waren
were

überbelegt
overbooked

sondern
but

auch
also

der
the

Raum
room

für
for

die
the

Aufbewahrung
storage

roter
of red

Farbe
paint

Deshalb
Therefor

wurden
were

solche
such

Eimer
buckets

über
over

eine
a

Menschenkette
human chain

an
to

Deck
deck

geschafft
worn

und
and

dort
there

entleert
emptied

Aus
From

den
the

leeren
empty

Farbeimern
colour buckets

wurden
were

Schuhe
shoes

hergestellt
produced

die
which

als
as

schwimmende
swimming

Wunder
wonder

beworben
advertised

wurden
were

und
and

von
from

oben
above

her
from

tropfte
dropped

beständig
steadily

ausgeschüttete
poured upon

rote
red

Farbe
paint

floss
flew

eigentlich
actually

in
in

einer
a

zähen
tough, sticky, *honey is ‚zäh',
but leather, too*

Masse
mass

die
the

Bordwand
board wall

entlang
along

auf
onto

‚meine'
my

Ebene
level

Dort
There

hielt
held

ich
I

immer
always

wieder
again

einige
some

Farbpaletten
colour palettes

an
on *(anhalten: to stop)*

konnte
could

aber
but

nie
never

einen
a

richtigen
richt, good, correct

Farbwert
colour value

ermitteln
determine

Dem
To the

Kapitän
captain

ließ
let

ich
I

deshalb
therefor

zukommen
(to inform, to bring a message to, to let bring a message to)

dass
that

es
it

wünschenswert
desirable

ist
is

dem
the

Präsentwunsch
present wish

einen
a

konkreten
specific

Farbwert
colour value

anzufügen
append

Wir
We

einigten
agreed

uns
us (on)

auf
on

$b91023
[value]

und
and

$b91024,
[value]

wodurch
whereby

Farbpaletten
colour palettes

als
as

solche
such

obsolet
obsolete

wurden
became

und
and

die
the

PassagierInnen
passengers, gendered

zumindest
at least

eine
a

kleine
small

Auswahlmöglichkeit
possibility to choose

hatten
had

Manche
Some

Gäste
guests

erlaubten
allowed

sich
themselves

einen
a

Scherz
joke, fun, hoax, frolic

und
and

brachten
brought

$42019b
[value]

oder
or

$32019b
[value]

mit
with them

was
which

in
in

einem
a

lilafarbenen
violet coloured

weiteren
further

Farbhügel
colour hill

mündete
resulted

Sie
You, *formal*

mögen
may

vielleicht
potentially

bemerken
remark

die
"The

beiden
both

letztgenannten
lastly named

Farbwerte
colour calues

sind
are

beide
both

dunkelblau
dark blue

fast
almost

marinefarben
marine coloured

aber
but

ich
I

kann
can

davon
of it

berichten
report

dass
that

die
the

EinlasskontrolluerInnen
entry supervisors, gendered

einfach
simply

die
the

gesamte
whole

Tranche
tranche, portion

aussortierten
to sort out

wenn
if

nur
only

einer
one

oder
or

zwei
two

der
of the

gleich
directly

nach
after

Einlass
entry

auf
on

einer
a

Palette
palette

gelagerten
stored

Farbeimer
colour bucket

nicht
not

rot
red

waren
were.

Die
The

Paletten
palettes

wurden
were

dann
then

per
using a

Kran
crane

nach
to, towards

oben
up, upwards

transportiert
transported

und
and

dort
there

entleert
emptied

Einmal
once

hatte
had

die
the

Reedereimitarbeiterin
ship owning company

die
the

Ineffizienz
inefficiency

kritisiert
critizised

die
which

durch
through

den
the

Luftwiderstand
aerial resistance

entstehe
emerged

weil
because

der
the

Kran
crane

zu
too

schnell
fast

führe
would drive, subj.

jedenfalls
in any case

schneller
faster

als
than

nötig
necessary

um
in order to

die
the

Farbeimer
colour buckets

auszuleeren
empty

Also
Concludingly

organisierte
organized

ich
I

durch
through

Gespräche
talks, conversations

mit
with

anderen
other

PassagierInnen
passengers, gendered

einen
a

zweiten
second

Kran
crane

denn
because

die
the

überfüllte
overfilled

MS
MS

daneben
beside

wurde
was

beständig
steadily

von
from

neuen
new

PassagierInnen
passengers, gendered

heimgesucht
to visit but knowingly damaging

Als
As

es
it

zu
to

regnen
rain

begann
began

platzierte
placed

ich
I

ein
a

schwimmendes
swimming

Wunder
wonder

verkehrtherum
invertedly

204

auf
on top of

meinem
my

Kopf
head

und
and

das
the

zweite
second

aus
from

dem
the

Paar
couple

auf
on

einem
a

vorbeilaufenden
walking by

Jungen
boy

mit
with

Schwert
sword

und
and

Kartoffelpellvorrichtung
potatoe peeling equipment

Später
Later

wurde
was

mir
to me

erzählt
told

dass
that

der
the

kleine
small, petit, little

den
the

Pool
pool

gefunden
found

hatte
had

und
and

zu
to

einer
a

großen
big

Suppenküche
soup kitchen

umorganisierte
reorganized

wordurch
through which

die
the

Bordpolizei
board police

eine
a

mit
with

Wasserspritzpistolen
water guns

ausgestattete
equipped

Vorstufe
pre-stage

der
of the

Bordarmee
board army

eine
a

Gulaschkanone
field kitchen

verschrotten
to scrap

konnte
could

Die
The

Bordarmee
board army

reagierte
reacted

darauf
on this

allerdings
but, however

mit
with

dem
the

Anbau
extension

zweier
of two

Schwimmkörper
swimming chassises, frames

die
which

jeweils
each

eine a	**Grundstock** basis	**wurde** became
wassergekühlte water cooled	**für** for	**fragte** asked
Kantine caboose	**die** the	**ich** I
enthielten contained	**hernach** after that	**mein** my
die which	**einlaufenden** running-in	**Spiegelbild** mirror image
im in the	**Köche** cooks	**ob** whether
Konfliktfall case of conflict	**dienten** served	**denn** ‚then' in the sense of ‚at all'
mit with	**Also** Thus	**das** the
Seewasser sea water	**war** was	**Wetter** wheather
gefüllt filled	**eine** a	**auf** on
werden to be	**Gulaschkanone** field kitchen	**der** the
konnte could	**durch** *through*, by	**anderen** other
wobei whereat	**zwei** two	**Seite** side
die the	**Fischsuppenküchen** fish soup kitchens	**besser** better
nach after	**ersetzt** replaced	**sei.** would be.
Entleerung evacuation	**worden** were.	**Das** The
zurückbleibenden remaining	**Da** As	**Spiegelbild** mirror image
Fische fishes	**der** the	**fragte** asked
als as	**Regen** rain	**mich** me
	intensiver more intensive	**gleichzeitig,** at the same time

wie how	**der** of the	**und** and
das the	**Reling** deck rail	**-decken** -ceilings
Wetter weather	**nicht** not	**fiel** fell
auf on	**nachließ** faded	**bis** until
der the	**und** and	**auf** on
anderen other	**stieg** stepped	**den** the
Seite side	**auf** onto	**Grund** bottom, ground
sei would be	**die** the	**des** of the
Ich I	**Streben** bars	**Hafenbeckens** harbour bassin
schaute looked	**der** of the	**Ein** A
nach up	**Reling** deck rail	**vorbeilaufender** walking by
sah saw	**verschwamm** blurred	**Junge** boy
dass that	**mit** with	**sagte** said
der the	**meinem** my	**in** in
Regen rain	**Spiegelbild** mirror image	**sogenanntem** so called
auch also	**das** which	**Bordchinesisch** board chinese
auf on	**danach** after that	**„Mann,** "Man
der the	**durch** through	**Reling,** deck rail
anderen other	**die** the	**Platsch".** splash"
Seite side	**Bordwände** board walls	**Fümmunzwanzigste** twentyfifth

Zäsur
Zaesuer

Auch
Also

das
the

Wasser
water

knapp
slightly

oberhalb
above

des
the

Hafenbeckenbodens
harbour basin

hat
has

einen
a

Promillewert
per mille value

Eigentlich
actually, *the plan differs*

hatte
had

die
the

MS
MS

daneben
nexttoit

„Phoenix
"Phoneix

MS
MS

&
and

Kreuzfahrten"
cruises"

heißen
to be called a name

sollen
sould have

aber
but

das
the

Völkerrecht
international law

sprach
spoke, stood against, would
have contradicted in court

dagegen
against it

Stattdessen
Instead

kam
came

es
it

also
~then, so, thus *(not ‚too')*

dazu
to it

dass
that

die
the

MS
MS

daneben
beside

durch
through

mich
me

getauft
baptemized

worden
had been

war
was

ein
a

einmaliger
unique

Umstand
circumstance

den
which

kaum
almost not, poorly

ein
a

Passagier
passanger

wahrzunehmen
to perceive

bereit
ready

gewesen
had been

war
was

andererseits
otherwise, then again

war
was

die
the

Taufe
baptism

der
of the

MS
MS

daneben
beside

auch
as well

gar
througoutly

nicht
not

angekündigt
announced

worden
was

Bereitwillig
willingly, unhesitantly

ersann
cogitated ~ invented

ich
I

eine
a

Realität
reality

in
in

der	**und**	**Pool**
which	and	pool
die	**zurück**	**an**
the	back	a
Phoenix	**nur**	**Bord**
Phoenix	only	board
MS	**um**	**der**
MS	in order to	the
&	**nicht**	**MS**
and	not	MS
Kreuzfahrten	**weiter**	**daneben**
cruises	further	nexttoit
mein	**an**	**der**
my	at	which
Vehikel	**den**	**sich**
vehicle	the	itself
war	**falsch**	**außerdem**
was	wrong	furthermore
Begeistert	**ausgeschilderten**	**an**
excited	according to signs	at
von	**Pool**	**Deck**
of	pool	deck
der	**denken**	**befand**
the	think	found, was placed
Idee	**zu**	**war**
idea	to	was
rannte	**müssen**	**nur**
ran	have to, would must	only
ich	**Den**	**erreichbar**
I	The	reacheable
vom	**falsch**	**wenn**
from the	wrong	if
Maschinenraum	**ausgeschilderten**	**man**
engine room	signposted	one
zur	**Pool**	**jedes**
to the	pool	every
Brücke	**der**	**Schild**
bridge	the	sign
	einzige	**das**
	only	which

den
the

Pool
pool

ausschilderte
signposted

absichtlich
intentionally, on purpose

falsch
wrong

interpretierte
interpreted

Das
That

war
was

auch
also, as well

der
the

Grund
reason

warum
why

man
one

im
in the

Angesichte
countenance; face, but very poetic

des
of the

Pools
pool

der
of the

MS
MS

daneben
beside

auch
as well

ein
a

Schild
sign

ansehen
watch

musste
had

auf
on

dem
which

zwar
other events occur

„Pool
pool

der
of the

MS
MS

daneben"
beside

stand,
stood

das
which

aber
but

in
in

die
the

Richtung
direction

zeigte
showed

aus
from

der
which

man
one

zum
to the

Pool
pool

der
of the

MS
MS

daneben
beside

gelangt
reached, arrived

war
was

Also
Thus

ersann
cognized, invented (inventing phantastic stuff like poems)

ich
I

die
the

Phoenix
phoenix

MS
MS

&
and

Kreuzfahrten
cruises

einen
a

eingetragenen
registered

Verein
association

wie
like

ich
I

herausfinden
to find out

wollte
wanted

und
and

wie
how

der
the

Fußballverein
soccer association

der
of the

Münchener
munich

Bayern
bavarians

Auf
On

der
the

Phoenix
Phoenix

MS
MS

&
and

Kreuzfahrten
cruises

e.V.
registered association
(abbreviation)

Inc.
~ GmbH

das
the

Schiff
ship

wurde
was

in
in

den
the

USA
Vereinigte Staaten von
Amerika

registriert
registered

wo
where

die
the

Steuern
taxes

auf
on

erträglich
tolerable

hohem
high

Niveau
level

den
the

ErbInnen
Inheritants, gendered

der
of the

Verschwörungstheorien
conspiracy theories

die
the

Illusion
illusion

geben
give

konnten
could

völlig
completely

machtlos
powerless

zu
to

sein
be

war
was

jedes
every

Rettungsboot
lifeboat

ein
a

Pool
pool

Im
In

Notfall
case of emergency

wurde
was

das
the

Wasser
water

aus
from

den
the

Rettungsbooten
lifeboats

herausgelassen
to let flow out

wodurch
through what

ein
a

schwimmfähiger
able to swim

Körper
body (alive), also structure with surface

entstand
emerged

der
which

das
the

mit
with

Wasser
water

vollaufende
to run full

Hauptvehikel
main vehicle

zu
to

ersetzen
replace

in
in

der
the

Lage
situation

war
was

Ausreichend
sufficiently

viele
many

Pools
pools

hatte
had

man
one

an
at

Bord
board

der
of the

Phoenix
phoenix

MS
ms

&
&

Kreuzfahrten
cruises

e.V.
registered association

Inc.
GmbH

Installiert
installed

aus
due to

kostengründen
cost reasons, efficiency etc.

waren
were

diese
those

aber
but

in
in

einer
a

Art
kind of

Wettercamouflage
weather-camouflage

gestrichen
painted

die
which

die
the

Außenfarbe
outer, exteriour color

der
of the

Pötte
ships, vulgar (big bowls)

stets
steadily

an
at

den
the

dahinterliegenden
lying behind, remaining behind

Horizont
horizon

anglich
align

So
Like that

waren
were

die
the

Pools
pools

nur
only

zu
to

finden
find

wenn
if

sie
they

korrekt
correctly

ausgeschildert
signposted

waren
were

Zu
At

Beginn
beginning

einer
of a

jeden
every (~of every single, but not diligently)

Kreuzfahrt
cruise

auf
on

der
the

Phoenix
phoenix

MS
MS

&
and

Kreuzfahrt
cruise

e.V.
registered association

Inc.
GmbH

wurde
was

folgende
following

Durchsage
announcement

an
to

alle
all, (not 'every')

PassagierInnen
passengers

weitergegeben
forwarded

Sehr
Very

geehrte
honored

FahrgästInnen
passengers, *gendered*

im
in the

unwahrscheinlichen
improbable

Notfalle
emergency

begeben
~to move within a situation

Sie
you, *formal*

sich
yourself

bitte
please

ruhig
silently, smoothly

und
and

ohne
without

Ihre
your

Accessoires
accessoires

zu
to

den
the

ausgeschilderten
signposted

Pools
pools

Handtücher
towels

liegen
lay

dort
there

für
for

Sie
you, *formal*

bereit
ready.

Wir
We

gehen
walk, leave

entweder
either

gemeinsam
together

Baden
to take a bath

Seite | page 117

oder	or
gar	(not at all)
nicht	not
Weiter	furtherly
wurde	was
dann	then
von	from
der	the
Reederei	ship owning company
durchgesagt	announced
wie	how
die	the
Allgemeinen	common
Geschäftsbedingungen	business conditions
lauteten	sound
»Sollte	should
die	the
Phoenix	phoenix
MS	MS
&	and

Kreuzfahrt	cruise
e.V.	registered association
Inc.	GmbH
sinken	sink
so	then
ist	is
die	the
Phoenix	phoenix
MS	ms
&	and
Kreuzfahrt	cruise
e.V.	registered association
Inc.	~ GmbH
kontrolliert	controlledly
zum	to the
Sinken	sinking
gebracht	brought
worden	was
Bewahren	Keep
Sie	you, *formal*

Ihre	your
Eintrittskarte	ticket
bei	close to
sich	you
Sie	you, *formal*
werden	will
im	in the
Falle	case
des	of the
Betreten	to step onto
eines	of a
Pooles	pool
danach	about it (in order to show it)
gefragt	questionned (to show the ticket)
die	the
Rettungsboote	lifeboats
sind	are
nicht	not
beheizt	heated

aber	**der**	**Wirbelstrom**
but	of the	turbulent flow, ~~whirl pool~~
die	**Phoenix**	**entdecken**
the	phoenix	discover
Pools	**MS**	**kann**
pools	ms	can
Vielen	**&**	**der**
many	and	which
Dank	**Kreuzfahrt**	**von**
thanks	cruise	from
Ihre	**e.V.**	**der**
your	registered association	the
Reederei	**Inc**	**Schiffsschraube**
ship owning company	~ GmbH	ships screw, propeller
PS	**befindet**	**verursacht**
postscript	befinds	caused
Farbeimer	**sich**	**aber**
colour buckets	itself	but
stehen	**achtern**	**nicht**
stand	aft	not
für	**das**	**behoben**
for	that	corrected
Sie	**ist**	**wird**
you, *formal*	is	is
am	**dort**	**im**
at the	there	in the
Ausgang	**wo**	**Falle**
exit	where	case
des	**man**	**einer**
of the	one	of a
Schiffes	**zum**	**Beerdigung**
ship	to the	funeral
bereit	**Wasser**	**werden**
ready	water	are being
Der	**herabblickend**	**schwere**
the	to look down	hard
Friedhof	**einen**	**Findlinge**
cementry	a	foundling, big stone
	wirren	**die**
	confused	which

im
in the

Verhältnis
ratio

1:0,5
1:0.5

Passagier:Findlinge
passenger:foundling

unter
under

Deck
deck

eingelagert
stored

werden
are

in
in

exakter
exact

Anzahl
amount

der
of the

betrauerten
grieved

dort
there

von
off

Bord
board

geworfen
thrown

und
and

über
over

die
the

Anzahl
amount

der
of the

Lebensjahre
life years

lang
long

ertönt
sounds

das
the

Schiffshorn
ships horn

Während
while

die
the

Findlinge
foundlings

die
the

Schiffsschraube
ship's screw

beschädigen
damage

bemerkt
notices

man
one

an
at

der
the

Brücke
bridge

einen
a

Geschwindigkeitsverlust
speed loss, loss of speed

der
which

in
in

einem
a

Gespräch
conversation

mit
with

dem
the

Maschinenraum
engine room

mündet
leads

Ein
a

ausgiebiger
extensive

Alkoholtest
alcohol test

aller
of a

BesatzungsmitgliederInnen
crew members

Crew
crew

bestätigt
confirms

dann
then

dem
to the

schiffseigenen
ships

Finanzamt
own

dass
financial office

entweder
either

ein
a

alkoholisierter
alcoholized

oder
or

ein
a

nicht-alkoholisierter
non-alcoholized

Geschwindigkeitsverlust
loss of speed

vorliegt
is on hand

Aufgrund
due to

der
the

Annahme
assumption

dass
that

stets
in every moment

mindestens
at least

zwei
two

falsche
wrong

respektive
respectively

blinde
blind

Passagierinnen
passengers

an
at

Bord
board

sind
are

lagern
store

einskommafünf
onepointfive

Findlinge
foundlings

in
in

der
the

Kajüte
cabin

des
of the

Kapitäns
captain

Apropos
apropos

Kapitän
captain

An
a

Bord
boatd

der
the

Phoenix
phoenix

MS
ms

&
and

Kreuzfahrt
cruise

e.V.
registered association

Inc.
gmbH

wird
is being

der
the

Kapitän
captain

auf
on

Basis
base

der
of the

vier
four

Grundsätze
fundamental assumptions

frei
freely

gleich
equally

allgemein
commonly

unmittelbar
directly, immediately

und
and

geheim
secretlyly

gewählt
elected

Die
The

Frage
question

welche
which

beiden	both
Grundsätze	fundamental assumptions
vor	in front of
dem	the
Hintergrund	background
der	of the
ethymologischen	ethymological
Identität	identities
„Republik"	"republic"
Res	res
Publika	publika
»öffentlicher	public
Gegenstand«	thing
äquivalent	equivalent
sind	are
und	and
deshalb	therefor
durch	through
einen	a
dritten	third
Begriff	term
ersetzt	replaced
werden	are, become
müssen	must
behalte	to keep (secret)
ich	I
Ihnen	you
vor	before (to not tell, rather)
Der	The
irische	irish
Reiseleiter	travel guide
beißt	bite
mir	to myself
in's	into the
rechte	right
Ohrläppchen	earlap
und	and
weckt	wakes
mich	me
aus	out of
meinem	my
Tagtraum	daydream
Sofort	immediately
alarmiere	alarmed
ich	I
mein	my
Spiegelbild	mirror-image
auf	on
der	the
anderen	other
Seite	side
der	of the
Reling	deck rail
„Sind	are
wir	we
vorhin	before
wirklich	really
von	off
Bord	board
gegangen	went

wie
how

der
the

kleine
small

Junge
boy

sagte
said

und
and

liegen
lie, floor position

am
at the

Grunde
bottom

des
of the

Hafenbeckens
harbour bassin

»Nein!«,
no

lasse
let

ich
I

mein
my

Spiegelbild
mirror image

antworten
answer

indem
in

ich
I

den
the

irischen
irish

Reiseleiter
travel guide

mit
with

den
the

sprachlichen
linguistic

Abwehrmechanismen
defense mechanisms

der
of the

hiesigen
around here, area around

Sprache
language

vertraut
not to find trust, but to get to
know familiarily

mache
make

»Yeah
toll

it's
das ist

good
gut

I'm
ich bin

okay«,
in ordnung

antwortet
answers

der
that one, the previously named
one

und
and

beißt
bites

in
in

ein
a

Wassereis
water ice

das
which

der
the

Form
shape

nach
relying to

mir
me

nachgebildet
recreated, cloned, but rather
'made in the same shape'

worden
had been

war
was

Mein
My

Oberkörper
upper body

verschwindet
disappears

in
in

seiner
his

Kauluke
mouth

und
and

220

ich
I

versuche
try

mich
myself

abzuwenden
to turn away

erstmals
for the first time

schaue
look, watch

ich
I

die
the

Reling
deck rail

in
in

die
the

andere
other

Richtung
direction

herab
down

und
and

erkenne
recognize

dass
that

sie
she

dort
there

entweder
either

noch
still

genau
exactly

einen
a

halben
half

Meter
meter

weit
far

reicht
reaches

bis
until

zu
to

einer
a

Bordwand
board wall

hinter
behind

der
which

sich
itself

offenbar
obviously

ein
a

Lagerraum
storage room

für
for

Rettungsringe
lifebelts

verbirgt
passes

oder
or

ein
a

bis
until

zum
to the

Fluchtpunkt
vanishing point

dessen
of that one

reichendes
reaching

Rätsel
riddle

darstellt
depict

das
which

zu
to

lösen
solve

mir
me

der
the

Reiseleiter
travelguide

ursprünglich
originally

in
in

eine
a

Vene
vene

gestochen
stitched

hatte
had

Gut
good

ok
ok

flüstere
whisper

ich
I

ohne
without

zu
to

wissen
know

ob
whether

mir
to me

jemand
someone

Aufmerksamkeit
attention

schenkt
to give

ich
I

nehme
take

das
the

Mandat
mandate

an.
to > to take: annehmen

Sofort
immediately

erscheint
appears

der
the

Kapitän
captain

vor
in front of

mir
me

und
and

versucht
tries

den
the

Pappaufsteller
paper cutout stand

in
in

Form
shape

des
of the

irischen
irish

Reiseleiters
travel guide

hinter
behind

seinem
his

Oberkörper
upper body

zu
to

verstecken
hide

was
which

natürlich
of course

insofern
insofar

zum
to

Scheitern
fail

„verurteilt"
judges

war
was

als
as

dass
that

beide
both

in
in

etwa
about, around

gleich
equally

groß
big

und
and

der
the

Pappaufsteller
paperboard cutout stand

in
in

Lebensgröße
life size

hergestellt
produced

worden
had been

war was	**Maschinenraum** engine room	**sank** sank
Pappaufsteller paperboard cutout stands	**das** the	**die** the
werden are	**komplette** complete	**Phoenix** phoenex
auf on	**Unterdeck** under deck *(level)*	**MS** ms
der the	**achtern** aft	**&** and
MS ms	**einnimmt** ~ to overspan, to take in	**Kreuzfahrt** cruis
daneben beside	**und** and	**e.V.** registered association
in in	**die** the	**Inc.** Gmbh
einem a	**schweren** heavy	**spontan** spontaneously
eigenen own	**Zylinder** cylinders	**vor** in front of
Raum room	**mit** with	**meinem** my
hergestellt produced	**entsprechend** corresponding	**inneren** inner
der which	**schweren** heavy	**Aug'.** eye
neben beside	**Findlingen** foundlings	**Den** The
dem the	**weiter** further	**Kapitän** captain
Maschinenraum engine room	**vorn'** in front	**informierte** informed
angesiedelt settled	**im** in the	**ich** I
ist is	**Schiffsrumpf** ships hull	**nüchtern** soberly
Da As	**ausgeglichen** balanced	**darüber** about the fact
der the	**wurden** were	**dass** that

er
he

sich
himself

in
in

einer
a

Straßenbahn
tramway

in
in

Richtung
direction

Vorstadt
suburb

jenseits
apart, beyond

des
of the

Stadions
stadium

aber
but

auch
as well

jenseits
beyond

der
the

Universität
university

nicht
not

aber
but, though

jenseits
beyond

der
the

Fachhochschule
specialized high school

befand
found itself

und
and

bald
soon

seinem
to his

grimmigen
ferocious

Vorgesetzten
boss, 'placed in front'

würde
would

begegnen
meet, run across, face

müssen
must

Andererseits
otherwise, then again

konnte
could

ich
I

mitteilen
inform, message

dass
that

eine
a

Woche
week

lang
long

den
the

Vorgesetzten
boss

zu
to

ignorieren
ignore

und
and

nur
only

zu
to

antworten
answer

keinen
no

Nachteil
disadvantage

mit
with

sich
itself

brächte
brought, would bring

was
which

die
the

Arbeitnehmer-/Arbeitgeber-Beziehung
employee/workgiver-relation; worktaker/workgiver-relation

betrifft
concerns

Sowieso
anyway

ist
is

in
in

der
the

Beziehung
relation

zwischen
between

Kapitän
captain

und
and

seiner
his

Reederei
ship owning company

das
the

Ablegen
departure

der
the

wichtigste
most important

Zeitpunkt
timepoint

Deshalb
thus, therefore

stehe
stand

ich
I

starr
rigid, inflexibly

an
at

der
the

Reling
deck rail

und
and

Blicke
look

auf
onto

den
the

halb
half

sichtbaren
visible

Fluchtpunkt
vanishing point

jenseits
beyond

der
the

durchsichtigen
transparend, see-through

Bordwand
board wall

»Interessant«,
interesting

murmelt
murmures

der
the

Reiseleiter
travel guide

und
and

summt
humms

die
the

irische
irish

Nationalhymne
national anthem

Kafkas
Kafkas

Leserschaft
Readership, group of readers

hatte
had

sich
itself

nicht
not

nur
only

für
for

dessen
his (kafkas), but especially not the second person ones (\ seine:his)

Texte
texts

interessiert
interested

sondern
but

produzierte
produced

selbst
itself

Text
text

der
which

die
the

Umstände
circumstances

Kafkas
of kafkas

Schreibnot
writing need, emergency, necessity, distress

zu
to

klären
clarify

als
as

Ziel
target

vorzugeben
to to pretend

schien
appeared

wobei
whereat

dessen
hes [kafkas]

Publikum
audience

nicht
not

exakt
exactly

jenen
those

Ziels
targets

bewusst
conscient

gewesen
had been

zu
to

sein
be

scheint
appeared

sondern
but

vielmehr
furthermore

es
it

als
as

Pflicht
duty

erachtete
consider

ob
facing

der
the

grauenhaften
horrible, morbid, atrocious

Texte
texts

selbst
self

aktiv
actively

zu
to

werden«.
become

»Nein«,
no

antwortete
answered

ich
I

und
and

bluffte
bluffed

eigentlich,
~ but not really

wusste
knew

aber
but

auch
as well

um
around

den
the

Umstand
circumstance

der
the

Ignoriertheit
ignorance

des
of the

Autoren
author

Kafka
Kafka

in
in

dessen
his

Findungsphase
finding phase

dass
that

also
as well

Kafka
Kafka

durch
through

sein
his

Schreiben
Writing

eine
a

Erkenntnis
finding, insight, cognition,

gnosis, awareness

hervorgerufen
induced

haben
have

muss
must

die
which

dazu
to it

führte
led

dass
that

seine
his

Lesendenschar
reading swarm

sich
itself

verpflichtet
committed

sah
saw

ebenfalls
likewise

so
in that way

wie
how

Kafka
Kafka

selbst
himself

Sečhsundzwanzigste
twentysixth

Zæsur
zæsoro

Kafkas
Kafkas

Werk
Work

war
was

unvollendet
incomplendet

und
and

das
the

obige
above

»čh«
¢h

möchte
want

ich
I

als
as

frigativlaut
scratching sound, to be
precised

interpretiert
interpreted

wissen
know

Satzzeichen
punctuation marks

in
in

das
that

Buch
book

passt
maches

ja
yes

überhaupt
at all

nicht
not

ŕein
int

Zäsur
break, censura

Siebenundzwanzig
twentyseven

Testtest
testtest

Ende
end

des
of the

Buchs
book

Bonusseite
bonus page

1
1

Malen
paint

Sie
you, *formal*

eine
a

Ente
duck

Bonusseite
bonus page

2
2

Kreieren
create

Sie
you, *formal*

eine
a

technische
technical

Zeichnung
drawing

Bonusseite
bonus page

2.1
2.1

Kreieren
create

Sie
you, *formal*

eine
a

weitere
further

technische
technical

Zeichnung   **T**
drawing   T

über   **r**
spanning over; over   r

zwei   **i**
two   i

Seiten   **c**
pages   c

hinweg   **k**
(away)   k

Bonusseite   **T**
Bonus page   T

2.2   **r**
2.2   r

Kreieren   **i**
create   i

Sie   **c**
you, *formal*   c

eine   **k**
a   k

weitere   .
further   .

technische
technical

Zeichnung
drawing

über
over

zwei
two

Seiten
pages

hinweg
a-away